MEMORIES O
KENT C

Martin Tapsell

Cinema, 49 St. Peters St. Canterbury

Plateway Press
13 Church Road, Croydon, CR0 1SG

British Library Cataloguing in Publication Data

Tapsell, Martin
  Memories of Kent cinemas.
  1. Moving-picture theaters—England—Kent—History
  I. Title
  791.43'09422'3   PN1993.5.G7

  ISBN 0–9511108–3–7

Printed in Great Britain by Whitstable Litho Ltd, Whitstable, Kent

Front cover illustration: In Kent, as elsewhere, the name 'Odeon', became synonymous with movie-going. The Odeon, Sittingbourne – seen here in 1937 – is a modest, but pleasing example of the Odeon style. (RCHM)
Frontispiece: A welcome from smartly turned-out staff like these – at the Canterbury Electric – was a normal part of movie-going between the Wars. (Author's collection)

CONTENTS

INTRODUCTION

In a densely populated county such as Kent, well provided with a varied selection of coastal resorts, the author expected to find no shortage of cinemas to write about. The final total of 172 nevertheless came as a surprise. Sheer weight of numbers dictated the exclusion of the areas now within the London boroughs of Bexley and Bromley, which must await a book of their own, alas. So many of the buildings used as cinemas were never intended for this purpose. We find diverse edifices conscripted into service, from Zion chapels to skating rinks and from theatres to oast houses. This variety and the range of well known architects who designed in Kent ensures that not even the purpose-built cinemas are uniform and predictable.

As 1987 proceeds, there is fresh optimism for the future of cinema in Britain, sustained by rising audiences and the first of the new multiplexes. However, there continue to be closures, and at the time of writing (summer, 1987) only 18 darkened places are left to carry the torch for big screen entertainment. The time to relate the story of what we have lost forever is obviously now.

Only an encyclopaedic volume could cover every detail of cinemas in such a populous county, so the author is happy to exchange information on individual places. Those who wish to see round cinemas and former cinemas are urged to join the Cinema Theatre Association, who have been arranging visits for 20 years. No book of this length could have been completed without the help of people still living in the county, whose personal memories or meticulous researches have proved invaluable. Of the latter, I owe a special debt to Tony Turner, whose extensive research notes are now deposited in Kent County Library HQ. Messrs Raymond Dolling and T. A. Thompson have also kindly placed their research at my disposal, whilst Clifford Manning and Tony Moss have done the same in the specialist field of the cinema organ. Many newspapers have carried articles, boosting my mailbag, and librarians have displayed posters or volunteered information. In addition, all the following have corresponded with me on at least one occasion: Frank Bangay, W. Michael Bishop, R.I.B.A., Laurie Brooks, Les Bull, Gillian Charlton, Gordon Church, Margaret Collins, Graham Cooper, Ronald Crosoer, Julie Deller, Mary Duck, East Kent Critic, John Emmett, R. H. Field, Ray Foad, Syd and Doris Goodsell, A.M. Grose, Mavis Hamblin, C. Holden, Ron Hull, Adrian Jackson, Arthur Johnson, Michael Kent, Derek Kiell, Mary Lilley, T. J. McCullen, L. C. Poupard, S. I. Robinson, Roger Simons, Doris Wilkins, David Willis, Guy Wrenn and Frank Wright.

Photographs are from the author's collection unless otherwise credited. Sincere thanks are due to organisations and individuals who have supplied photographs. The abbreviations 'CTA' and 'RCHM' indicate the Cinema Theatre Association and Royal Commission for Historical Monuments respectively.

MARTIN TAPSELL
89 Welbeck Avenue, Aylsebury, Bucks. HP21 9BL
June 1987

ASHFORD

Sundry halls and theatres of varying sophistication played host to the newborn cinematograph. Only the evident success of the medium and parliamentary legislation, induced local businessmen to erect the first electric palaces. ASHFORD followed this pattern, where the Norwood Street Drill Hall was pressed into service for twice weekly film shows from the 22 November 1909. Success paved the way for the **Ashford Electric Picture Palace**, Tufton Street, which was built in 1911 for the Ashford Entertainment Co. A. E. Lacey's arched entrance, reminiscent of the surviving Plaza, Margate, was flanked by a shop on each side, with a paybox facing the street in early cinema style. A terrazo mosaic paved reception hall led through pairs of swing doors to a wedge-shaped auditorium, 50 ft wide at the back. The 600 seats were leather-covered downstairs, but in green velvet in the gallery. The stalls floor was raked, and the box had the obligatory fireproof walls. At the opening on the 18 December 1911, colour was provided by crimson carpeting, but the onset of winter postponed the decoration of the interior, including the arched elliptical ceiling, for several months. Despite a power failure at the second house, the EPP soon caught on, sufficiently to justify an orchestra pit being excavated in front of the screen. Talkies came with Western Electric and 'The Singing Fool' from the 11 November 1929, and business continued for almost another ten years. Acquired by the East Kent Cinema Co., the cinema, now plain 'Palace' finally surrendered to younger competition on the 22 July 1939, closing with 'Zaza'. Kent Paper Co. moved in until 1956, but now a branch of Courts marks the site.

Mr Lacey also designed the Royal Cinema de Luxe in Beaver Road. This was the ancestor of the present **Picture House**. The original cinema at the top of New-town Road had a stepped frontage with niches and ledges for tubs of shrubs. A wrought-iron canopy over the two main entrances announced: 'Living Pictures – Royal Cinema de Luxe – Dramatic and Operatic'. The interior consisted of a vestibule, main hall and balcony (total seating 1,050), seats all being velvet blue and gilt tip-ups. 'West End' standards of decor included gilt mirrors, and after drying out, an auditorium in royal blue and gilt, with a night sky ceiling. Following theatre tradition, the rear stalls were cheapest, whilst balcony patrons were served coffee daily from 4 p.m. Attendants, male and female, wore Quaker costumes. The stage, large enough for 80 to 90 artistes, had a shell-shaped roof to improve acoustics.

At the opening on the 24 June 1912, music was provided by the De Luxe Cabinet Orchestra, directed by Maisie Brook. A dozen choirboys provided vocal support for the film 'Christopher Columbus' and to mark the first night, lady first nighters were given a free fan. The stage was mainly used for Sunday concerts, whilst the 21-foot screen, kalee machines and sound effects machine took over on weekdays. In 1917, a 3-manual straight organ was built for the De Luxe by Vincents, who included 18 speaking stops, bells, drums and cymbals. The prefix 'Royal' was dropped in the thirties, and in 1935, the architect E. A. Jackson was engaged to remodel the building. A new thirties style front was put on including the present corrugated corner feature. Inside the shell, the auditorium was modernised with coves for concealed lighting and the ante proscenium walls painted in foliage patterns.

The reconstruction complete, it was **'The Cinema'** which resumed on the 14 January 1936, now seating about 1,000. By the fifties, the Cinema was being run by Jack Croneen (q.v. Gillingham) and was very little altered. In 1975, Rank tried to buy out Croneen, but failing to do so, converted their Odeon to bingo. When Mr Markwick took over in 1983, he wanted to twin the Cinema, but found that costly rewiring was a priority, and followed up by attention to seats, broken stalls, flooring etc. Redecoration of the frontage and some modernisation of the foyer and circle lounge followed, namely carpeting, painting and spotlights. At this stage the shabby walls of the auditorium had the 1935 foliage decor intact, and capacity had fallen to about 690. Phase 2 was achieved around April 1985 when the Cinema was twinned, greatly reducing heating costs. It was also renamed **Picture House** and became a triple in May 1987.

Andrew Mather's **Odeon** at 35 High Street was a 1,570 seat cinema with a restrained brick frontage that has weathered 51 years well. The vestibule led to a long foyer decorated in green, gold, red and black with stairs on the left side to the café/ballroom overhead. Four hundred and sixty-eight of the patrons could ascend staircases to the circle with effect from the 31 August 1936, the remaining 1,102 occupying the stalls. The band of the 1st Battalion, the Royal Scots invited to play on this occasion were no doubt as 'one hundred percent British' as the cinema itself. The programme continued with Gaumont British News and the film 'Strike Me Pink'. The BT-H and other apparatus high up in the box was kept in immaculate order throughout the Odeon's history, whose success was greatly enhanced too by enthusiastic managers like 'Bamps' Bampton. Bamps, who died in retirement in 1979, made the cinema's presence at carnivals and other fund-raising events a matter of course. Apart from films, the café and ballroom, known latterly as the Kent Suite, was bookable for private functions – early booking advised!

Ten thousand residents signed the petitition to retain the Odeon as a cinema, but the continuing competition with the Croneen Cinema was producing a corresponding £10,000 annual deficit. Thus the last two films – 'The Four Musketeers' and 'Magic Dream' played here on the 30 August 1975. Top Rank bingo has been in residence ever since the 29 January 1976, although many locals still call the club 'The Odeon'. The auditorium is largely unspoilt, except for sales kiosks flanking each side of the proscenium and the usual tables for bingo in the stalls. The projection box is a store, whilst the Kent Suite has adjusted to the times, being leased out as a disco, with a licensed bistro of cosy proportions adjoining. One entity ignores the times however. The ghost of a worker at an iron foundry which once stood on part of the site, can still be heard, not seen, after the bingo players have left. The temperature is said to drop in the stage area and the foundry worker makes his clanking way across the cinema.

The Cinema, Ashford, in 1985 (Kentish Express)

The Odeon, Ashford, in 1936 (RCHM)

TENTERDEN had a thoroughly disinfected **Cinema Palace** standing in Oaks Road from 1912. This 'fine picture theatre' held 350 and was run by Albert Harry Pollard, who had other halls in Rye and Hastings. At one time, all the staff came from the Verden family. The Palace commenced operation on the 28 September and ran uneventfully until it was superseded by the Embassy. After closure, a series of lock-up shops was created along the side wall of the cinema, and there appears to have been a one-floor extension beyond the original frontage. The Fairings still stand.

Hastings architect H. W. Coussens, designed the **Embassy** on a central High Street site (south-east side). Externally not unlike the Majestic Sevenoaks, it was an example of the tasteful cinemas built by the Shipman and King circuit whose heartland was the country towns of south-east England. The futuristic carpeting in wine-coloured hues drew comment at the opening, as did the lighting fixtures in red and clear frosted glass. 'Windbag the Sailor' was the film chosen for the first show on the 11 February 1937. A first floor café, homely rather than elegant, completed the amenities.

A small 800 seat super cinema, the Embassy remained with the same chain (S & K), until closure in 1969. Two thousand signed a petition to retain the cinema when rumours of a supermarket takeover broke, but takings were insufficient. Theatre controller, A. E. Randall said: 'This closure is a great pity. We have been in Tenterden for many years'. Vyes the grocers gutted the interior, but retained the name on the frontage. We understand that demolition is now likely.

The Embassy, Tenterden, c.1965 (R. P. Crosoer)

CANTERBURY

West's animated coloured pictures were included in a variety programme at the St Margaret's Hall, **CANTERBURY**, as early as Boxing Day, 1903. A freemasons hotel and two halls stood in St Margarets Street, the lesser being used as an auction mart. From the 8 November 1909, the larger hall was rented by Robert and Lloyd Forsyth of the Victoria Pier, Folkestone, as an electric picture palace. A sheet-metal box was perched on the roof, in which films often broke. The venture was further capitalised by the forming of the Electric Picture Palace (Canterbury) Ltd., in February 1911, chaired by William Henry Court, the furnisher. Pathe Imperial machines were bought in November, but the competition from the Canterbury Electric Theatre caused films to be dropped in September 1912. A few were exhibited after the hall was used as a YMCA from the 11 December 1914, but until its demolition, the building operated as the Empire Music Hall.

The **Canterbury Electric** had opened at 49A St Peters Street, on the 1st June 1911. Its slogan was: 'If our programme pleases, tell your friends, if not, the manager'. The electric was purpose-built to the design of F. H. Dore and A. R. Bowles, the latter conceiving the lovely ornamental glass canopy over the entrance. There was a central paybox with an oak panelled corridor leading to the 520 seat auditorium. This boasted a balcony, tip-up seats and a tea bar open between 4 and 6 p.m. Dark red carpeting and electric lighting with pretty silk shades and bead fringes were also noticed by the press. Continuous performances reigned until the Central cinema opened, the last show here being on Guy Fawkes night, 1927. Interestingly, the Electric next traded as the Odeon Hall or Odeon Music Hall, then from the 31 August 1936, as the Canterbury Repertory Theatre. After the war, the old cinema became Perry's Talisman restaurant, in which dayboys from King's School lunched until 1960. For the last two decades, the fare has been chinese. The owners of the Lok Yin (House of Happiness) have put in a false ceiling, obliterating any hint of cinema, but the ladies toilet is still in the old balcony.

At nos. 12–13 St Georges Street, another early cinema arose in 1911. W. R. Sprague's **Palais de Luxe** claimed it could be emptied in only 30 seconds in case of fire. Otherwise, patrons could admire the quaint De Jong and Co. Dutch decor. Renamed the Canterbury Cinematograph Theatre in February, 1913 when H. G. Wilson took over, the cinema soon succumbed to competition, closing early in 1915. The site was used by David Greig (grocers), but was destroyed by bombing in June 1942. The **St Georges Theatre** in Lower Bridge Street superseded the old Palais, its name recalling the erstwhile gateway. Designed as a cinema-theatre by Jennings and Gray, it was compact and not over ornamental. A corner entrance in Bridge Street led to a circular vestibule. The auditorium itself had walls of fibrous pink plaster, a raked parquet floor, red Sheraton-style chairs, a first floor tea room and a circle (200 seats), with rear promenade. The theatre opened with a film – 'A Patriot of France, or The Ordeal' on the 8 February 1915, but the Old

Stagers and Canterbury Operatic Society also played here. Ecstatic advertising greeted the booking of 'Ben Hur' in January 1928, a foretaste of further hype in 1930. RCA sound was then installed in time for a showing of 'Phantom in the House' on the 22 December. Two super cinemas (no less), caused the last film advert to appear on the 12 May 1934. In 1936, the Co-op bought the building for a store, but a dance hall was opened on the second floor. The latter was disabled by the war. Road widening finally disposed of the whole building in April 1961.

The aforementioned Empire Music Hall came down in 1926, to be replaced by the **Central Picture Theatre**. This was erected on behalf of Canterbury Electric Theatre Co. to the design of H. Anderson (of Dore and Anderson, Canterbury). Half-timbered, Tudoresque, gabled and casement windowed, with a vestibule panelled in dark oak, the new cinema seated 735, 235 of these in the balcony. The interior decor was Wedgewood blue with white fresco work. The two kalee machines had a 100-ft throw to the screen, commencing with the film 'The Somme' from the 7 November 1927. W. T. Mainwaring and his staff were there from the Canterbury Electric. By 1930, citizens were complaining about travelling to the coast to witness talkies, so finally on the 19 May 1930, MGM's all-talking, all-singing dancing sensation, 'Hollywood Revue' came to Canterbury. To the relief of the Western Electric engineer, the sound conversion was an acoustic success.

The Central joined the ABC circuit in September 1935, and only 2 months later, were permitted to screen Sunday films. In wartime, the cinema was twice hit, closing the second time for 5 months until the 22 March 1943. The last show ran on the 18 September 1948, after which the City Council, inspired by the Festival of Britain, purchased the property for £20,000. L. Hugh Wilson, the city architect, was engaged to convert the cinema into a civic theatre, adding stage facilities at the rear. Thus the Marlowe Theatre came into being on the 29th May, 1950, staging 'The Chiltern Hundreds'. For 32 years, the Marlowe entertained Canterbury with rep or latter-day touring companies, nude revues and celebrity shows. Money was tight, audiences small and acting within such strict confines difficult. Mary O'Hara gave the Marlowe a musical swansong on the 22 May 1982, after which demolition men were the next act on stage. A draughty shopping complex now marks the site, but at least by 1982, the agonising was over – Canterbury was to get a replacement theatre.

Marlowe Theatre II is also a former cinema. Back in the thirties, both Charles Donada of County and Oscar Deutsch of Odeon considered Canterbury needed a super cinema. The race to provide one proved a draw, for on the 5 August 1933, not one but two new cinemas opened! The Friars Theatre in The Friars, claimed to be in harmony with the ancient city. Unlike Odeon's later faience palaces, architects Alfred and Vincent Burr came up with a slightly ponderous but symmetrical building on the site of Binnewith House. The auditorium was lit by cornice lighting and shellac plaster features, and seated 1,291, including private boxes at the back of the stalls and 413 seats in the circle. The writer of the opening programme enthused about the secluded position with flower garden

The Friars (later Odeon), Canterbury, c.1934 (RCHM)

The Compton organ at the Canterbury Regal (John D. Sharp)

11

in the forecourt and the age-old trees. An oak standard stood in one flower bed supporting an antique lantern. The name 'Friars' above the canopy instead of Odeon was due to the failure of negotiations with the Odeon Hall only some 200 yards away. After a short-lived attempt in April, 1938, the cinema only became the **Odeon** in December 1955. This cinema was the author's local for many years, and he recalls being able to leave his cycle unattended for 3 hours in the car park to the rear, without any misgivings at all.

Lt Col William Wayland, M.P., performed the opening ceremony, at which the main feature was 'I Lived With You' Oscar Deutsch was in the audience to mark the opening of only his fourth purpose-built cinema. The pace was later to quicken considerably! Organless, the Friars booked the Reg Elton band for 6 months to compete with the Regal. Between them, these cinemas induced city cinemagoers to part with £1,200 a week, compared with £275 a week at the 3 older cinemas. (Oscar Deutsch, 1935). Besides films, the cinema hosted the Miss Canterbury competition, and later relayed broadcasts of 'Six-Five Special' a BBC precursor of 'Top of the Pops'. In wartime, the ATC occupied the cellar whilst the verandah served as a lookout. Takings fell in the sixties, despite the new university. Matinees were cut back, the last childen's Saturday morning show came in 1978, and the last of many live shows on stage was David Essex, who played the Odeon on the 5 October, 1981. Unsuitable for subdivision, the circuit added this cinema to a list for closure in the autumn of 1981. On a suitably dull Saturday (17 October) a depressing film called 'The Janitor' played out the silver screen in this building. After a spell of disuse, the City Council gave the go-ahead for the purchase of the Odeon as the new Marlowe. A much altered and extended theatre re-opened on the 27 September 1984, in the presence of the Duke of Kent. There is now a single rake seating 986, with a long bar across and underneath the old rear stalls area. Some German-made chandeliers and cloud effect walls transform the interior whilst a new flytower and glazed side entrances massively augment the bulk of the building. Marlow II cost £2¾ million.

Regal (Canterbury) Ltd's theatre opened at 43 St Georges Place, as soon as the mayor, Alderman Frank Hooker had arrived hot-foot from the Friars. He found Robert Cromie's 'contemporary medieval' style suitably regal, and was no doubt impressed by the trumpeters of the Coldstream Guards, followed by County's musical director, Reginald Foort at the 3-manual 9-unit Compton. A Walt Disney Silly Symphony, a Magic Carpet story and British Movietone news all preceded the main feature – 'Falling For You'. Guests were then entertained at a reception in the adjoining ballroom. The **Regal** also had a first floor café with Lloyd loom chairs. The original capacity was 1,750. From the outset, the Regal was managed by Donada's burgeoning County circuit, but before County ran into difficulties, this cinema was taken over by ABC from the 29 April 1935. Wartime brought disaster, for as soon as patrons left the matinee of 'Gone With The Wind' on the 31 October 1942, one of 190 Focke-Wulfe bombers wrecked the rear of the cinema, adding the café and ballroom to the toll next day. Organist Tom

Williams, at that time in khaki, was there at the time. His Compton survived, but truncated and off balance, the Regal stayed closed until February 1943.

Post-war, the Regal organ fell silent, and thirty years on, the name changed to **ABC**. Next year (1964), Brian Pritchard arrived as manager, and tried some publicity stunts – police were called when 2 'Nazis' were seen at the station! Late night kung fu films were attracting Chinese from all over East Kent until videos became available. After a 3 month conversion, a circle only ABC re-opened with 'Joe Kidd' on the 24 October 1972. Five hundred and thirty-six could see a film, and 758 could scan bingo score cards in the stalls. A separate cinema entrance had to be created beside the existing one. On the 50th anniversary, Canterbury ATC provided a fanfare for the sheriff who had driven up in a 1929 saloon, whilst 50 quiz winners saw 'Superman' free. Today it is not the ABC plus EMI Bingo, but the **Cannon** Cinema plus Coral bingo. EMI mercifully had tastefully redecorated the cinema in 1984, picking out the barleycorn in gilt. Lest I forget, Stan Port rescued the organ at time of twinning, and took it away to Rochester Organ Studios for restoration.

The City acquired another cinema in a building adjoining the University's Cornwallis building, from October, 1969. It was first known as the Canterbury Film Theatre, in view of its BFI status and programming, then Cinema 3, ranking third after the ABC and Odeon. The cinema is a public one, advertising in the local press, and seats around 300. It is equipped with 35mm and 16mm.

HERNE BAY, like Canterbury, had several early film venues. The Town Hall (1859) at the junction of High Street and William Street ran films from the 15 May 1911, with free tea in the best seats. By 1912, it was using the name **Grand Cinema**, spelt out in no less than 292 lights. Under various lessees film shows continued until the Town Hall was gutted in 1925. Even earlier, films had been shown in the Pier Pavilion Theatre and the St Georges Hall, Sea Street, both from 1910. Then amber, ruby, green and blue fairylights enticed patrons through the coved entrance of Pettman's **Paragon Cinema** at 19 High Street. This hall measured 100-ft by 18-ft wide and seated 300. A projection box lined with sheet iron contained a Maltese Cross lantern supplied with power from an 11 h.p. Stockport gas engine. This was coupled to a Holmes Castle dynamo. The auditorium was painted chocolate up to dado rail level, then pale pink, broken by chocolate panels. This early hall ceased trading as a cinema during the Great War but was last heard of in use as the Kent Trailer Centre.

Better known and also still standing is the former **Red Lantern Cinema**, 75 High Street. Originally opening as the Cinema de Luxe on the 7 August 1911, it was rapidly altered by architect J. Wilson and recommenced again on the 19 August, 1912 as the Bijou Theatre. As such, pictures, variety and concerts were offered, but in 1926, Archibald Iggulden became the proprietor and the name Red Lantern was coined. The last event of note was when Union cinemas acquired both the Lantern and the Casino, early in 1936. Unprofitable off season, Union sought to close for the winter from September, 1937, but the cinema probably did not open the following May as expected. The building had been a clothing

A 1930s view of the Red Lantern, Herne Bay

factory – Thanet Clothing then Townbrook Manufacturing – and until recently a shop known as Spender's Arcade. The high concave entrance with original glazing survives, as does the word 'pictures' set into the plasterwork. The shop ran back to the edge of the balcony, with surviving cinema decor highlighted and even an old price tariff on the wall.

Much less can be seen in the amusement arcade that was the **Casino Cinema** 55 Central Promenade. It opened on the 26 May 1919, and had to drop plans for a tea lounge due to the current shortage of labour and materials. Afternoon teas, dances, concerts, cabarets, and whist drives were put on initially as well as films. After the Union chain acquired the Casino, and modernised and redecorated the interior, reopening on Boxing Day, 1936 with 'Wolf's Clothing'. The cinema now seated 708 on one floor, and was ultra plain apart from some grille work. The box had BT-H and Zeis Ikon machines later superseded by RCA sound and Simplex projectors from the Broadway, Hammersmith in 1952. The 1953 floods closed the Casino for 3 nights from the 31 January until enough seats had dried out. ABC, who had inherited the property, closed it down altogether in October 1954. Derelict for over 2 decades, the Casino narrowly avoided redevelopment in 1974, but is now partly used by an amusement arcade who have put in a false ceiling.

Closer to the centre, the **Odeon**, Avenue Road, was designed by Andrew Mather and opened on the 2 November 1936. Built in 2 shades of cream brick with stone dressings, the squared-off corner entrance had an illuminated metal grille displaying an Octagonal O for Odeon. This was painted into a C when Classic took over! The Odeon seated 974 on a stadium plan. Its first performance featured the Royal Marines band and the feature 'Where There's A Will'. Manager George Stanton, showed the will, founding a children's circle who greeted him in the street with the call 'Hi te hi!' Still little changed, this was one of the cinemas Odeon disposed of to Classic in late 1967. Classic spent £15,000 which included a tower projector with xenon 2½ KW pressure lamp, replacing the secondhand carbon arcs obtained from Gateshead in 1960. Although good attendances were reported as recently as 1984, Cannon ceased advertising programmes in the press late in 1986 and the local film fans are uncertain about the future of Canterbury district's only seaside cinema.

WHITSTABLE has no film audiences at all now, since the **Oxford** turned to bingo only from the 5 October 1984. The name Oxford is venerable, for the Oxford Animated Picture Hall opened in the Parish Hall on the 16 July 1910, in time to show the funeral of Edward VII. Children were favoured with free matinees and bars of 'picture hall rock'. For 9d., adults could have a curtain drawn round them, to reduce draughts not for privacy! From the 11 December 1912, a purpose-built hall with scrolled and glazed canopy, opened on the present site. The interior had a heavy plaster cornice and carved capitols.

In 1936, the walls of a new cinema were built – engulfing the old one. The balcony cleared the roof by about two inches and still the show went on. After a minimal gap of 3 weeks, the new Oxford was ready. Designed by local architect

The Oxford Picture Hall, Whitstable, c. 1922 (Douglas West collection)

W. M. Bishop, the enlarged cinema seated 850, and was faced in multicoloured bricks and snowcrete rendered blocks. There was an illuminated name sign, whilst inside lighting was indirect in current fashion. The decor was coral and gold, with oak lining for about 6 feet up the walls. From the opening film on the 27 July 1936 (Jack Hulbert in 'Jack Of All Trades'), the Oxford stayed out of the main circuits. Part-week bingo was introduced around 1962, and by 1980 only some 394 seats were in use. In 1981, ownership passed to Fawrona Ltd., Rochester, and 3 years later it was decided that even after subsidisation by bingo, films were unviable. Only 3 patrons and a Whitstable Times reporter were there to see 'Blame It On Rio'. As a touch of nostalgia, veteran projectionist Wally Dukes played an old ABC disc released in 1965 – 'Curtains And Lights'. So far it has been curtains for films, although Wally would like to see the projection equipment used again.

Near the Victoria/Harbour Street intersection, 2 shops – a butchers and a grocers both called Ganns – were adapted by W. G. R. Sprague into a none-too palatial cinema. 'Always showing, no waiting' the hall boasted. A man called Edwin Chinnick stood outside this **Palais de Luxe**, calling 'My people, step inside'. Pictures and variety could be enjoyed here until about 1931, after which the hall was used by a furnishers. The High Street **Picture House** was a little more grand, having the services of the Whitstable String Band. Designed by Edwin Pover, it opened on the 26 February 1913, offering everyone a clear view of the screen. In March, patrons could see 'A tour through Whitstable, including scenes of famous artist Daniel Sherrin at home'. The cinema was an adaptation of Church & Co.'s furniture store, with elaborate heraldic motifs in relief on the façade. Patrons passed to the right of the paybox, finding the screen at the High Street end. Henry Paton, the proprietor, also built radio sets, and listened to the early 2LO broadcasts from London.

Rebuilt like the Oxford, it was F. E. Bromige who designed the 1,000 seat **Argosy** on this site. Another non-circuit house, the Argosy was equipped with Zeis Ikon sound and later RCA. The main event was a remodelling in late 1950, which took only 18 days. The charioteer frescoes may date from that time as they were certainly there to witness the 1953 floods. The remodelling justified a name change to **Regal**. The manager at the time, B. E. Fortescue, had started his career as a page boy at the Palais de Luxe. After cinemascope was installed in 1954, seating capacity fell to 936. However, the last owners (Highland Development Trust, whose cinemas were almost all in Kent), sold out to a supermarket chain in 1960. By then one cinema sufficed for the town. 'This Wonderful Country' closed the Regal on the 17 September 1960, after which Fine Fare gutted the interior. For a time, a chinese restaurant occupied the former circle lounge area. The supermarket continues.

TANKERTON had the largest cinema of all, the **Troc**, not Trocadero. Another local architect, Major W. Puttick designed this building as a skating rink with maple floor. Whitstable had won the world rink hockey cup but the craze faded, and the building had to be expensively adapted into a talkie cinema. The reinforced concrete construction made alterations impossible and the owners, Tankerton Grand Pavilion Co., had to provide extra generators to power the 130-foot throw to the screen. Major Puttick died before the Troc opened on the 9 February 1931. Three thousand people saw 'Dawn Patrol' in the first two houses. The building abutted some tennis courts at the Whitstable end, but patrons entered through a foyer on the ground floor of a residential block facing Marine Parade. I would estimate capacity at 1,500 inclusive of 250 in the balcony, seat rows being originally over 3 feet apart. During a fire on the night of 9/10 December 1938, firemen forced an entry through the café. W. M. Bishop, who had designed the Oxford, was called in and recalls a brick wall was dropped down the middle of the building to cut the projection throw and improve the suitability of the place.

The Troc was back in business on the 19 June 1939 with 'The Advent Of Robin Hood'. Vivacious Miss Rona Kennett had risen from usherette to manageress by the age of 25. Closed in 1947, the Urban District Council declined to take over the Troc, and so Harry Reynold Productions moved in the following year, taking out some seats to make room for film studios. This led to some redecoration and new heating. However, on the 3 January 1949, the cinema re-opened briefly as the **Embassy**. However, the company decided to concentrate on revamping the Argosy (q.v.) so the Embassy closed on the 20 August 1950. This was still not the end, for in November, the cinema was back as the largest 16mm static in Britain! Debrie Cinetechnic machines were brought in and Rank personality Barbara Murray came to the 16mm launch. The final curtain came only a few months later. Subsequently the building has been used partly by the fire service and a toy manufacturer. The foyer was left empty in the midst of the flats. A municipal sports hall scheme was mooted in 1978. The firemen were reportedly disturbed by ghostly organ music according to a Cinema Organ Society Newsletter, but as there was no recorded organ at the Troc, this does seem beyond the usual range of the spirit world!

DARTFORD

DARTFORD's proximity to London may have encouraged the early arrival of cinematograph exhibitors. The Conservative Club in Spital Street was booking Poole's Myorama in March 1909, and Dan Barnard's Music Hall, began by booking the bioscope at the 8th turn in the second rush. By 1915, 3 years later, Kellys describes the place as Barnard's Imperial Bioscope! One source describes a 'white-fronted cinema' in the High Street where Marks and Spencer now stands, with a domed paybox and chairs linked by deal planks. This was probably Ruffel's Bioscope, in existence by 1907, the year it engaged Francis Chiodini as violinist. On screen, these pioneer audiences would watch scenes of the breakwater at Jeu de Crux in rough weather, or follow Arabella's misfortunes as a domestic on roller skates.

The first real cinema however, was the **New**, Lowfield Street, which opened on the 19 November 1913. This was Richard Lovell's fine building, with turreted frontage and wide glass canopy to shelter those queuing at the central paybox. The foyer was paved in mosaic, from which patrons ascended a marble staircase to the 995 seat auditorium. The side rows were innovatingly angled for a better view of the screen. There were panelled dado and side walls under a curved ceiling. For musical entertainment, both a grand piano and pipe organ were provided. In 1926, Dartford Cinema Co. redecorated the interior, installed tub seating, raised the height of the screen and installed dimmers for the house lights. After passing to Medway Cinemas, the name changed in 1933 to Rialto. Granada followed suit from 1947, and they chose The Century – (a name they used when already having a Granada in a town) – with effect from 1952. The Century did not close for lack of custom, but because an irresistible offer was made for the site. After the last showing of 'The Bells Are Ringing' plus 'Balloons And Spinifex' the screen went dark on the 29 October 1960. Soon a Shoppers Paradise supermarket replaced it. Perhaps its main claim to fame was the New's experimentation with sound in the form of the kinetophone as early as November 1914. Also it had the flamboyant Mrs West as manageress in the early years – one who ejected troublesome male patrons in person. This was at a time when women managed very little outside the home.

Another lady ran the **Gem Picture House**, Spital Street, which occupied a site adjacent to the later Granada. Mrs A. D. Tong had charge of 750 seats (stalls and balcony), with stage and dressing rooms. The Gem opened sometime before the Great War, taking up the greater part of the Constitutional Club. In 1915, Sunday performances were permitted, for the duration only, but did not resume again until after a poll taken in November 1932. A rare memento of the Gem is kept in Dartford library, namely a souvenir blotter dating from 1921, which packs in advice on medical preparations, household hints and names for babies. It also claims the Gem had a good orchestra and a 'programme properly projected onto the sheet'. The exact closure date is uncertain, but in 1943 the whole building was up for sale for redevelopment. Traces of the old Gem can be seen still at the rear of Courts the furnishers.

The **Scala** at the junction of Kent and Essex roads is still with us. Opened as late as the 30 November 1921, the proprietors still provided stage space in case the films did not pay. The opening film, 'The Tavern Knight' was surprisingly about Cromwell! Fog held up some last minute seat deliveries, but initially, the Scala held 800, until a balcony holding 200 more was put in. By 1938, all 3 main cinemas were run by Medway Cinemas, but after the last war, the Scala became a live theatre, opening as such on the 27 October 1947. TV was to hit attendances, and from March 1952, there were a series of closures and reprieves. In 1963, Irishman Bill O'Sullivan transformed the shabby cinema into a ballroom, laying a new maple floor for 500 dancers. Joe Loss and his orchestra were persuaded to forgo their usual day off and play at the opening on the 4 March. Wrestling, boxing and dining were the new combination at the Scala, but Mr O'Sullivan's 5-year lease from the council was not resumed, hence we find Keam Investments running a bingo club here in the seventies. Although some patrons found the atmosphere more intimate than the more lavish Granadaclub, the needs of the younger set for a social venue ultimately prevailed. A night club took over in late 1978. The current name 'Flicks' is a nice gesture towards the flickering screen which used to entertain inside this much altered building.

Dartford's last cinema, the **State**, was purpose-built for Medway Cinemas. A fanfare from the Scots Guards on the day before Christmas Eve, 1935, heralded the opening. Designed by J. Stanley Beard and W. R. Bennett to hold 1,500, the State in Spital Street had a front elevation in terracotta flanked by brickwork. Inside, the balcony had a cantilevered 63-foot span overlooking a classical style auditorium, decorated in beige and antique bronze with gold and green highlighting. The proscenium arch was flanked by splayed walls with a continuous grille edged off by stencil designs. A 3-manual 6-unit Compton, with lift, illuminated console and melotone was played mainly by Reginald New until 1940. The chambers were located under the stage. Lewis Gerard came to broadcast from this Compton whilst serving in the police war reserve at Grantham. He was later to become musical director for the States Dartford, and Grantham, and also the Capitol, Wembley. The organ's worst moments came much later during the floods of September 1968. The pipes swam in a mixture of mud and oil, but undaunted, James Crampton of Oxnead, Norfolk, renovated the instrument, and minus the illuminated surround, it was rendered fit for a new home at the Gunton Hall Country Club in Suffolk from 1979.

The State's opening and closing films make a good contrast – there were 50 years between Victor McLaglan in 'The Informer' and 'Barry McKenzie Holds His Own'. Despite being built over a stream and the consequences in 1968, the State flourished, joining the Granada circuit from the 24 October 1949, after which it became The Granada. This circuit installed cinemascope at a cost of £7,000 in 1954. Two years on, manager Dan Sullivan began to entice the young with Sunday evening disc shows. The younger still had their Grenadier club on Saturday mornings – films and organ interludes by Douglas Sharp. Parents found the cinema a useful childminder and their offspring watched endless

The State, Dartford, in 1982 (Tony Turner)

The Jubilee, Swanscombe, c. 1935 (R. H. Simmons)

Captain Marvel adventures and short documentaries. With low admission prices and annual birthday cards for each member, the Grenadiers were almost a social service. In the seventies Granada calculated that 7,000 bingo players could replace dwindling film audiences. From the approach to the Gaming Committee in May 1973 until victory on appeal to the Secretary of State in 1975, much opposition had come from the Council, the Dartford Society and the Scala, but less from the community. Thus on the 28 June 1975, the Granada ceased to be a cinema. Now, instead of the Granadaclub, the modern Orchard Centre near the station is the place to find an evening's film entertainment.

SWANSCOMBE, like Northfleet, replaced its first cinema with a new one, this time on the exact site. The *Gravesend Reporter* mentions an **Electric** cinema in the issue dated the 17 February 1923, although an article on the social life of Swanscombe only 2 months later makes no mention of cinemas. Apparently the Electric was run by Mr Mercia, who ran a hardware and paraffin store. His daughter Connie not only served in the shop but played the piano at the cinema. I am informed the building was of corrugated iron and called, unofficially at least, The Mercia. Poor ventilation was known to fog up the projection ports, so at intervals, the back row had to be cleared in order to wipe the ports clean! From about June 1935 the cinema was patriotically renamed **The Jubilee**, having called itself The Tivoli immediately prior to that. In 1939, however, the building was razed to make way for the more up-to-date Wardona.

Designed by Thomas Braddock of London WC2, the **Wardona** seated 550 on one level, and boasted: 'Every seat an armchair, deep upholstery, fully sprung, no class distinction'. Externally, the front was plain, except for a fin at the right-hand end on which the name Wardona blazed in neon. Billboards illuminated by spotlights covered wall space over the canopy. The local paper pictures the cashier behind her plate glass on the right-hand side of the fern-bedecked and chequered floored foyer. She is also shown admiring herself in an oval mirror inside the ladies cosmetic room. The auditorium had a curved roof echoed in the proscenium arch with its ribbed surround. Otherwise the decor was simple and no doubt standard Wardona.

Dartford M.P. Jennie Adamson performed the ceremony on the 3 July 1939, at which the preliminaries included a trumpet fanfare from the First Northfleet Scouts and music from Roy Siville and his Racketeers. Then Gaumont British machines brought 'The Lady Vanishes' and 'Say It In French' to the screen. Harry Ward promised more delights to come with a Wardona Kiddies' Cub to open that Saturday. The cinema opened daily at 1.45 (7.30 on Sundays). But the small town locations ensured that all the Wardonas caught a chill in the fifties, and here the illness proved terminal on the 28 March 1958. The cinema was used for warehousing although bingo was mooted in May 1974. The site in Ames Road has been cleared for some years now and is earmarked for sheltered housing.

DOVER

Despite its status as a major port of entry bustling with visitors, **DOVER** today lacks the cinema one would expect in a more conventional seaside resort. Before the Great War however, matters were completely different. 'A dreadful little fleapit' (to quote one resident), was opened on the 25 February 1911 as **Shanly's Electric Theatre**. This occupied the Wellington Hall, Snargate Street, formerly a navvies' mission. Shanly, a London bioscope proprietor, refurbished the hall in Egyptian style. His opening films, ticket only, were the edifying 'Bill's Redemption' plus 'Waffles Tries Work'. Fleas notwithstanding, the cinema flourished, calling itself the Wellington Hall in 1922, and the Pavilion from February 1930. However, shortly after New Year's Day, 1931, the hall closed, supposedly still a silent house. Until destroyed in wartime, it was used as a public hall.

Further along from no. 21 Snargate Street, at no. 52, was another hall – the **Apollonian** – forming an upper room in a hotel of the same name. Despite standing at a busy tramway curve known as Court's Corner, it was less successful as a cinema. Opened also in 1911, the name was originally The People's Picture Palace. Inside the PPP, a lady thumped the piano as a man prompted the people to sing lustily by prodding the words on screen with a black stick. The long vanished Apollonian played host to films for only a few years. By 1925, the hotel owners, Kent Brewery Co., used the room for dancing.

The **Queens Hall**, Queen Street was no palace, but showed better fare, including the early cartoon 'Felix The Cat'. The hall was a former Zion, later Congregational chapel, built in 1703. Two hundred and six years later, it was prepared for opening as a 500 seat cinema on the 27 December. Electric Pictures (Dover) retained the side galleries on their flimsy pillars, plus the main gallery facing the pulpit. There was a foyer, with, to the right, a narrow passage with separate paybox for 'the circle'. Entry was by token, holes having been punched in them. The patron had a programme to read at the next available interval. Talkies made the Queens obsolescent, and so it closed on or near the 8 April 1933. It became a leather shop, but the site at the junction of Last Lane was redeveloped in October 1974.

The fourth and leading early cinema was the **Kings Hall**, 49 Biggin Street. Messrs Pessers, Moodie, Wraith and Gurr had formed the Dover Picture Palace Co., who engaged A. H. Steele to design their hall. It measured 100 by 60 feet and seated 800 inclusive of the balcony. Some double seats were appreciated by courting couples. Opened on the 21 October, 1911, the Kings duelled in the press with the rival Queens who undercut them by a bottom price of 4d. However, the Kings had a resident orchestra and a Gregorian organ for your extra pennies. There was also variety, which took up sole residence for a time in 1913. Harry Day's Amusements took over in 1917, and lessees Dover Entertainments made some improvements in the twenties. After only 2 days to reseat and recarpet the Kings, it reopened on the 22 December 1929 as a theatre.

Talkies were soon beckoning however, so after RCA had wired up for sound, it was 'Madonna Of The Streets' ushering in a talkie cinema on the 6 April 1931.

The observant will notice that the brickwork hardly appears to be 1911 vintage and this is explained by a fire of massive proportions on the 29 December 1937. Everything perished, but plans for a new cinema holding more at the expense of stage space, were given approval in March 1939. Rebuilding was completed for Keystone Cinemas, despite the war, but the building became a naval gunnery school. They must have used blanks, for finally in 1947, by now under Odeon Theatres, the cinema was able to welcome queues four deep to see 'Frieda' on the 14 July. 'Would you accept a German girl into your home?' asked the posters of passers-by, including German P.O.W.s. The re-born steel-framed cinema held 1,050 and yet retained a large stage. It was still the Kings Hall, but became the **Gaumont** in January 1951, there being an Odeon in town already. Films played on until Rod Taylor bade farewell in 'The Time Machine' on the 26 November 1960. First Top Rank and then Zetters took advantage of the legislation of bingo. Today it has a mix of 3 periods; a narrow richly ornamented and gabled frontage recalling its origins as the Central Temperance Hall; thirties entrance and interior designed by Frank Verity and Samuel Beverley; and the autumn 1986 refurbishment by Zetters costing £250,000 to bring their 3,500 patrons the latest comforts of a modern social club.

Behind Zetters, you can spy the more venerable brickwork of the old **Plaza** Cinema, 20 Cannon Street. Below the brick wall, a sign reminds us: 'The unrecorded history of Dover, Kent and Britain lies buried here'. On the surface however, bingo plays quietly on. The premises originated as part of the Metropole Building, consisting of a bar and billiards rooms. The Plaza, whose name is recalled by the tiles at the entrance, was just in time to show a silent film on its painted screen. On the 1 July 1929, it was Chaplain in 'Shoulder Arms' plus 'Does Mother Know Best?' and 'Life's Mockery'. However, the *Dover Express* announced 'Blackmail At Plaza' referring to Hitchcock's talkie which ran from the 25 November. The 1,200 seater was owned by a syndicate, Messrs Solly, Overs and Barnard, and managed by ABC. Off screen drama occurred when Manager George Roberts was killed by an axe and his body dumped in the basement. An operator at the Plaza confessed, but the Home Secretary commuted his death sentence to penal servitude.

Designed once again by A. H. Steele, the Plaza had a fan-shaped auditorium and a sliding roof. The delay in converting to sound during 1929 is explained by Western Electric's quote of £500 plus 50% of takings. The management stalled but finally went for RCA photophone instead. Both management and name changed to **Essoldo** in 1952. By 1960 films were supplemented by wrestling, but when late in 1967 the floor was levelled and 200 seats in the front stalls were removed, we can assume that only bingo players sat in the remaining 700 seats. The latter-day visitor will find a passage painted orange, with a blue ceiling, besides Milletts store. At the end of this a sign saying 'Guinness on draught' glows silently, but it is to be hoped that there is enough interest in bingo to keep both Rio Bingo and Zetters bingo alive in Dover, thus preserving both of these buildings. In the words of the sign at the back: 'A country which destroys its past deserves no future'.

A tram ride in the Canterbury direction took Dovorians to the **Buckland Picture House**, 225 London Road. This 533-seater often changed hands after opening on Boxing Day 1920, hence the new name **Regent** in 1923. The decor was plain but pleasing, but in the words of the last proprietor, Arthur Phillips, the capacity inadequate. Not inappropriately therefore, 'The Imperfect Lady' closed down the first Regent on the 31 May 1936. I understand that it was designed by Worsfold and Hayward and was approached by a garden pathway at the front.

Ten months later, another **Regent** stood on an adjacent site. This was opened by Lord Willingdon, Lord Warden of the Cinque Ports,on the 27 March 1937. Much larger with 1,800 seats and a stone and black faience front, the Regent had air-conditioning, concealed lighting and Western Electric Mirrorphonic Sound. There was also a full stage and dressing rooms, but no organ. Richard Arlen starred in the opening film, 'The Great Barrier'. Before being acquired by Odeon in July 1943, the Regent belonged to Universal Cinema Theatres and Anglo-Scottish Theatres. Although further inland, the roof was hit in the war. However, the Regent (**Odeon** from January 1946) was not too disadvantaged by the suburban location until business slumped in the sixties.

After the Gaumont became Top Rank bingo, 'a warm welcome awaits you at the Odeon' but in 1968 plans for bingo were announced here as well, 'just as insurance'. However, the insurance policy did not mature for nothing followed the last act on screen. 'Tom Jones' romped off the screen on the 2 October 1971, and the Odeon waited for the demolition squad for 5 years and one month. In June 1980, a modern Albuhera Drill Hall took up position at the end of the raised terrace and this is home for a volunteer company of the Queens Regiment. The handiwork of Percy Kelly and Kenneth Winch of Elgood and Hastie is no longer part of London Road, Dover.

Signs began to appear on tram buffers during 1929, reading: 'Start saying Granada' – no explanation, but it transpired that Sidney Bernstein had been on a walking tour of southern Spain and had chosen the name **Granada** for his Dover cinema. It sounded better than County Theatre and Tea Room, so Bovis built the first of the Granadas with Cecil Massey as architect and the famed Theodore Komisarjevsky as designer. Staff recruited were expected to be 'intelligent, speak good English, have a very smart appearance and have good teeth'. Anything less would be unworthy of the Moorish palace which the whole town came to gape at in Castle Street. There was a lofty entrance hall, overlooked by a balcony with carved stone balustrades. Adjectives used included 'gay without gaudiness and magnificent without ponderosity' and 'the Russian Ballet's dream of a Moorish palace'. The inner vestibule had a large cut-glass chandelier, Spanish shawls hanging from the balustrades and a wide staircase on one side. The auditorium was decorated in shades of red, gold, green and yellow, and one could also admire the Japanese lacquer of the fine 3-manual 7-unit Christie organ.

The opening night audience were amused by the tableau on stage of architect, clerk of works etc. all busily wielding quill pens next to a blackboard commanding: 'The Granada must be open by January 8'. It was ready, so Norma Shearer starred in her first talkie 'The Last Of Mrs Cheyney' with Mickey Mouse, Pathe Pictorial and British Movietone News in support. So were Hedley Morton at the organ and an orchestra under Leonardi, who had been an infant prodigy on the violin. Technically, the Granada had Western Electric sound, Ross projectors and the latest Plenum apparatus. The grilles to the right side of the proscenium concealed the organ pipes.

When Leonardi and Hedley Morton moved on in 1931, Granada had to lower their prices, but stage shows resumed in 1934 when Stanley Amos was organist. In July 1935, Granada disposed of this cinema to ABC, as Dover lacked the audiences of larger resorts. However, the name Granada only changed to ABC in April 1960. From April 1935 until his retirement in September 1957, manager Sydney Sale played host to many ABC executives passing through the port, and raised funds for many local charities. Thereafter, as audiences fell, the balcony was closed and the decor repainted in chocolate, to conceal the scale of the cinema from the 610 persons occupying the stalls. Clive Batten tried out late night shows and competitions, and there were requests to EMI to twin this ABC as late as 1981. However, high youth unemployment and the video boom took business away, so the ABC ran into the buffers with 'Pink Floyd, The Wall' on the 30 October 1982. Mr Batten went to the ABC, Bexleyheath and the chief, David Robinson to the ABC, Canterbury. In June 1984, a nightclub called Images was opened by David Chalk. There are two dance floors, the larger one nearest the screen (in situ). Lighting alone cost £20,000. Charleston type furniture and art deco set the mood. On my visit, the nightclub ran from 8 p.m. until 1.45 a.m. Wednesdays to Saturdays, with Kate Wolfe's aerobic classes on the floor on Wednesdays.

Last in Dover itself there is the **Town Hall**, which with about 650 seats, showed films as early as October 1897. Films must be 'non flam' and shown by special licence of the Council. Because of other use, the Town Hall had not been licensed to show films in the normal manner of cinemas. Moving pictures also played a small part in the life of the Royal Hippodrome, Snargate Street (1897–1944) whose 800 seats were emptied by a direct hit from a wartime shell on the 18 September 1944.

'As from the 31 January (1985) this cinema will be closed for good' read the notice on the Classic, **DEAL**, but fortunately this was not so. However, we can confidently assert that the Assembly Rooms (1795) are gone for good. Famed for supper dances and balls, Charles Collins converted the building at the corner of High and Duke Streets into a cinema. From the 11 April 1910, the **Marina Picture Hall** opened its doors, offering free parking – it was bath chairs and cycles rather than cars that were envisaged. Patrons paid 6d or 3d for admission, for 6d occupying a raised platform at the back. A year later, electric light was installed. Mr Collins, a native of Ilford, personally introduced his films, adding his own quips and comments to the action, whilst his daughters Sybil and Lizzie sold the tickets and Frank Pocklington played the piano. A kamm, a wrench and an Urban were essential for the projection of the pictures, whilst a 6½ h. p. gas engine with a Crompton Dynamo were initially responsible for supplying the current. Sometime late in 1913, all this equipment fell silent, and the hall became a corn store, latterly for T. Denne & Sons. Clarence Place now occupies the site.

As films had to be bought outright in those days, Mr Collins had the motivation to re-exhibit them at the Royal Marines Garrison Theatre, Canada Road from November 1910. Here a change of programme was made twice a week and a slightly higher charge of 9d made to reserve a seat in the orchestra stalls. From the 3 August 1912 a third outlet opened in the **Kings Hall**, WALMER. These premises in New Barrack Road were designed for Collins company, Deal & Walmer Amusements, by C. L. Crowther of Deal. The Kings was built of brick with stone dressings, the name in gilt lettering on the pediment. The auditorium seated 344, mostly in rexine seats, with a single row of green velvet ones behind them. The threepennies had a separate entrance in York Road. The Kings was ventilated by 3 bullseye windows on either side and had gaslit exit signs. The decor was a sandwich of chocolate to dado level, pale green then deep crimson from the plaster moulding up to the roof. In World War II, the name changed to Ace, management being based at the Ace, Queenborough, but latterly the name Tivoli was used. 'Rookies' was the last film to play on the 23 March 1949. The Strand Palais dance hall took over from the 19 October 1950 and continued into the sixties. The Rolling Stones played there in both 1961 and 1962. The cinema became a car showroom, the old corner entrance given over to viewing the latest automobiles inside.

Back in DEAL, the **Queens Hall**, later **Plaza**, still stands, but the shop blinds obscure its origin. The High Street/Stanhope Road property dates from 1911, opening then as the Queens Hall Picture Palace on the 11 September. George Charles Brown managed the cinema for most of its life on behalf of Queens Cinema Co. The company were based in Folkestone and also operated in Ramsgate. There is some evidence that they showed films for a time at the Pavilion on the old 1864 pier, which seated 500 after an enlargement in 1897. Be that as it may, the Plaza was the new name for the Queens when it became Deal's first talkie house from the 16 June 1930. A.W.H. sound and a new screen were installed to cope with 'Hollywood Revue'. However, competition from later cinemas eventually proved fatal, as the Plaza closed very quietly on the 2 January 1937. It became a 50/– tailors, and is now divided into small shops. Four stone balls on the parapet are there for those who look up.

Also early in cinema terms, was the fourth building to receive the attention of Charles Collins. Before closing the Marina, Deal & Walmer Amusements had installed an 18-foot screen in the Theatre Royal, King Street. Built in 1890–91 for the Palmerston Lodge of Oddfellows, the theatre originally presented concerts, plays and pantos. The 'largest screen in the district' brought different fare. The Royal Marines band were close at hand to accompany some of the finer epics

The Odeon (later Classic), Deal, in 1936 (RCHM)

The Regent, Deal, after conversion to Bingo (CTA)

28

presented. A real crush materialised in July 1930, when a month after the Queens, the Theatre Royal presented the talkie 'All Quiet On The Western Front'. On one night even the projectionist could not get in! Between the 31 October 1933 and the 12 February 1934, H. W. Coussens of Hastings was brought in to replace the old wooden balcony with one on a steel and concrete span. The open truss roof was covered with fibrous plaster and the stalls seating set back to increase capacity to 616. Plenum ventilation and Ossicade deaf aids added to patrons' comforts. The re-opening film in what as now The **Royal**, was 'Henry VIII'. The history of the cinema after that can be summarised as bingo between October 1961 and July 1963 and then films again until 'The Mirror Cracked' on the 4 April 1981.

By 1981, Deal seemed lucky to have two cinemas, and the older Royal gave way to use as an amusement arcade downstairs. The view from the balcony seats is on to a false suspended ceiling revealing the top half of the festoon curtain. On the stairway, a gas light, 'Gone With The Wind' poster and a fine etched window showing a desert island scene, add interest. Some GK equipment survives in the box, with little economic prospect of re-use.

Bingo finally settled in the larger and thus more suitable one-floor **Regent**, Victoria Parade. This has a seaside pavilion look, borne out by its origins as a council owned pavilion built in 1928. Lord Warden, Earl Beauchamp performed the opening of the Pavilion Theatre on the 28 July, but hopes that good quality stage shows would prove viable were soon dashed. Instead the Borough Council leased the Pavilion for cinema use at a rental of £550 per annum. Architect P. Levett of Margate realigned the seating to face west instead of south, and a new 15-foot deep brick-lined stage replaced the iron and glass work at the west end. One thousand patrons could now enter through the flush burr walnut doors with their chromium plating. The box was sited in a first floor extension, with rewind and battery rooms, and manager's office at opposite ends of a corridor. The new name Regent blazed outside in multi-hued neon, whilst the internal decor was green and old gold, the staff also wearing green uniforms. There was a café and 2 dressing rooms, the former now used as a bar for bingo patrons immediately to the left of the foyer. All was ready for 'King Of The Ritz' (not the Regent) on the 13 July 1933.

Films finally died at the Regent when the Bloom Circuit found that the Royal could not cope with bingo, and so the town's only seafront cinema had to welcome the bingo caller. 'The Secret Mark Of D'Artigan' marked closure as a cinema on the 13 July 1963. Bingo remains today, with a false ceiling hiding the ribbed and barrelled roof. The original proscenium arch is behind a wooden scoreboard screen. Some original GB seats linger on at the back.

The **Odeon** has weathered badly in latter years, emphasising the decline of cinema in Deal. Built on the site of Admiralty House, Queen Street, this stadium style cinema was opened by the mayor of Deal on the 25 July 1936. Designed by Andrew Mather, it held 922, and was described by Mayor J. G. Tooms as a 'distinct indication of the increasing importance and development of Deal'. Mrs

29

The Empire, Sandwich, in 1937 (CTA)

Oscar Deutsch, wife of the chairman and a guard of honour from the British Legion were there to agree with him. Although the roof was blown off in an air raid on the 11 August 1942, the Odeon was back in business with 'Let The People Sing' on the 6 September. Charles Stead had founded a flourishing Saturday morning children's club back in 1937. Their parents were able to drive into the 200 space car park through an arch to the right of the entrance doors.

Disposed of to Classic in December 1967, the rising chain were intent on increasing business by creating the first twin cinema in Kent. The result was not ideal, the 2 auditoria, both seating 284, were too long and narrow and acoustically unsatisfactory. The twins opened on the 30 June 1972, leaving the Odeonesque projection room much the same, apart from new ports to serve the two screens. The £50,000 conversion was put in jeopardy by the economic recession, worsened in 1984 by the effect of the miners' strike. The work of manageress Jean Bailey and her staff seemed all in vain when she put up that closure notice. However, one screen reopened on the 11 September 1986, trading as Flicks. The man to thank is manager/projectionist Alexander Wallace, formerly manager at the Royal. Now part of an entertainment centre, the cinema provides a home for 173 cinema fans.

Early cinema in **SANDWICH** is obscure. Messrs Claringbould and Goodwin had brought pictures to the New Inn Assembly Rooms, from November 1911. Under the name **Empire Electric Theatre**, the pictures moved during the Great War to premises in Delf Street. Meanwhile, an Elite Palace of Fun existed a few yards from the Barbican gate. This was entertaining troops during the Great War and may be the same building referred to in the same area by Kellys 1918 directory as the **Picture Playhouse**. If so it was no palace, and all the buildings on the east side immediately before the Barbican were pulled down in 1926. The original **Empire** was small with a level floor, except for a raised platform at the back. Despite frequent breaks in projection, the hall lasted until the thirties, but probably not until a new Empire was designed at no. 15 Delf Street for S. Goodman. This vast advance upon earlier provision was designed by Alfred and Vincent Burr (Odeon, Canterbury and Australia House). A steel framed structure with brick infilling, the Empire had a metal and glass canopy with the letter 'E' for Empire in aluminium. Inside, the auditorium seated 600, inclusive of balcony, and featured some attractive old gold proscenium curtains and silver festoons. The spacious box was equipped with BT-H sound.

On opening night, the 26 June 1937, the films chosen were 'Trust The Navy' and 'Craig's Wife'. Like its forebear, proprietors changed quite often, the Empire joining the Southern Cinemas chain, based in Ryde, Isle of Wight, during the fifties. When the nearby R.A.F. station closed in 1956, business faltered. The Empire closed for the winter on the 28 October 1961, but next summer, the lessee George Edwards tried part-time bingo. That November, the Sandwich Town Council took the bold step of taking over the cinema under a cinema committee. The Borough Surveyor acted as manager, but R. H. Field, of the Carlton Westgate, was consulted on booking policy. Some art house programming replaced bingo for a time, but from February 1966, score cards were back on Mondays, and from May, on Fridays too. To enhance cinema, new projection, amplifiers and sound equipment had been installed in 1963, and prices were cut from 3/9d and 3/– to 2/6d or 1/6d. However, films faded away, ceasing altogether in September 1971. Bingo ran on alone for a decade more, after which the displaced players were bussed to the Rio (ex Plaza) Dover. The Empire is now being refurbished as a snooker hall, though provision has been made for a small (140 seat) cinema in the former circle area.

A surprising discovery just outside Sandwich was the wartime cinema at **Lord Kitchener's Camp, RICHBOROUGH**. With funds from the Odeon chairman Oscar Deutsch, refugees from Nazi Germany converted a derelict building into a 600-seat cinema. It opened as such in Deutsch's presence, during June 1938. Mrs Lionel de Rothchild declared it open after the camp orchestra had played the National Anthem. Presumably the cinema closed as the refugees moved away from a likely invasion zone.

Miners in the pit village of **AYLESHAM** were told by Aylesham Tenants Ltd that land was too costly for a cinema to be provided. By 1930, however, the village had grown to 502 houses, so a cinema was provided in Grace Road, opening in November 1935. Seating 394, the plain brick building was equipped with Kalee sound and open nightly except Wednesdays. The cinema came to be called the Chipper, after proprietor Arthur Chipper. By 1964, however, films had totally given way to bingo.

The Cinema, Aylesham, little altered as a bingo hall (CTA)

GRAVESHAM

A short walk around **GRAVESEND** reveals 4 surviving buildings in close prox-imity. Even with Bejam in residence, the origins of their New Road premises as the Public Hall (1878) are clear. Films came to the upper hall in 1910, prospered and moved next year to the larger lower hall. Now known as the Popular Picture Palace after the company which we shall also encounter in Maidstone, a January 1911 press advertisement explains that films would be shown on weekdays, and sacred vocal and 'pictorial' concerts on Sundays. Edwin Britnell, who had come to the town to play with the Royal Sparks at the Concert Pavilion, now directed the PPP's fine orchestra. Audiences were sold penny programmes listing the films by number, and at 10 minute intervals the lights came up, enabling them to follow the programme. The longest ever serial of 30 two-reel episodes started in 1915, but was not concluded before the Popular became the Palace Theatre. Poor acoustics ruined business and it was the Palais de Luxe cinema trading here in 1919. After closing briefly, the nearby Gem's management took over, christening the hall the Empire Picture Palace. Attempts were made to upgrade the film fare, such as a part week share of Chaplin's film, 'The Kid'. However, standards fell away and the orchestra was replaced by a pianist. Next the Empire traded as a silent western specialist, but the supply dried up in 1930. After a shot at being the Rivoli Music Hall for only 2 months, the premises stayed empty until rescued by Union Cinemas.

Union took over the **Regent** (another name!) on the 3 of November 1932, and tried a policy of 4 hour programmes with 2 main features. The jinxed cinema failed to respond, so A. H. Jones was engaged to carry out an internal recon-struction. The opening programme of the enlarged 954 seat **Super Cinema** described it as 'unique', meaning perhaps the peach and silver decor, simplicity relieved by the elaborate fluted procenium arch. There was also a 3-manual 5-unit organ with a 'cascade' illuminated console. Lewis Gerard was engaged at the Compton to follow on from the first day guest player, Alex Taylor. As it happens, an earlier instrument had sat briefly in the gallery, but was soon removed – it was those awful acoustics again. A gala ceremony to relaunch the Super took place on the 16 Sepember 1933, at which Anna Neagle was present. Western Electric sound brought a superior rendition of 'Cavalcade' but the Super was also to book live acts. Billy Cotton and Donald Peers were among the latter. Months after its silver jubilee the inheritors of the Super, ABC, decided Gravesend did not need three cinemas, so closed it down with Kenneth More in 'Next To No Time'. This occurred on the 23 November 1958. Bejam and Vincent's Diner are now in residence, but the first floor level is tastefully preserved. The organ had long since left for the Ritz, Scunthorpe during 1936/37.

The **Plaza**, Windmill Street is least recognisably 'cinema' today. Opened as plain The Cinema on the 19 July 1911, it was too late to show George V's coronation, so substituted the Prince of Wales' investiture! The Cinema was quite comfortable for the day, with raked floor, carpeting and brass ashtrays attached to the seats. R. J. Lovell's interior was finished in cream and fawn, with solid oak dados and crimson panels. Someone accidentally switched off two roof fans, so the first nighters sweltered before the 19 by 14-ft 'sheet'. Continuous performances in the London fashion played at the Cinema under the management of the Gravesend Picture Co. The name changed only once – to Plaza after RCA sound had been installed. The conversion included some costly 1½ cwt accumulators. 'Broadway Melody' was the talkie booked from the 16 September 1929. Union took control here in 1934, closing the Plaza for the last 3 weeks in September. However a longer 7 month break was dictated by a fire in July 1935. As an ABC house, it was a case of 'if you miss it at the Majestic, you can pick it up at the Plaza'. Not after the 12 March 1955 however. Passers-by today must look out for Toppers dress shop, or pass through a side passage to Fishers hairdressing saloon. Some 744 once sat where ladies now seek after fashion, but it is 32 years since the last sortie of 'Khyber Patrol' and even longer since Martha, the ghost who crashed the seats, last put in an appearance.

The **Gem Picture Theatre**, 65 New Road, was last to open before the Great War. Charles Lovell this time was engaged on this larger cinema (750 plus 330 in the balcony). This included 2 boxes for six apiece at the front corners. The entrance hall was flanked by pillars, arches and statues, and tiled in a floral pattern. Both here and in the lounge tea room, old rose and white panelling was employed, whilst the auditorium was painted out in Wedgewood blue hues. The Gem opened on the 1 October 1910, maintaining throughout the silent era, its masthead slogan: 'Home of famous plays and celebrated orchestras'. There was indeed space for a stage, yet the fine orchestra seemed a big enough draw in itself. With the gifted Florence Vincent as pianist, the orchestra could often eclipse the films. The renters provided detailed cue sheets for the musical director, or entire scores for major films. Talkies understandably came late, on the 15 December 1930 to be exact with a BT-H rendering of 'Sky Hawk' and 'Rogue Song'. Once again, Union took over on the 23 December 1933. Their choice of name was **Regal**, used from the 7 May 1934. As the number 2 ABC house, films played on until the 10 August 1968. A free bingo game with a £100 prize tempted the new users inside. First it was EMI, now Coral. The auditorium is kept in good decorative order, although the boxes have been removed.

The last survivor is the **Cannon**, formerly the **Majestic**, 11 King Street. The Gem Theatre Co. engaged George Clay from a still surviving firm of architects, and his workmanship was ready by the 1 October 1931. The classical façade of Portland stone now displays a Cannon vertical sign in place of ABC. The original entrance was paved in black and white marble or coloured marble for the wainscotting. Main features in the auditorium (1,838 seats) were the oval dome under the balcony, which housed concealed lighting and doubled as a ventilation outlet. There was Hollophane lighting, BT-H sound, Kalee 8s and the 'world's first Trenbex screen'. This could expand up to 44 feet wide. A café, now disused, was situated over the foyer. The scale of this all British enterprise is revealed in the opening programme, for example 1,000 cubic feet of sand and ½ million bricks

A 1930s view of Gravesend's Super Cinema (CTA)

The Majestic, Gravesend, in ABC days, c.1963 (CTA)

were used to render the cinema fit to exhibit 'Rookery Nook'. Two years on, a new company was formed to run both Gem and Majestic, with Mr Tong, chairman of the old Gem Theatre Co remaining. Various improvements such as a new stage and better entrance lighting were made in advance of the Union takeover on the 23 December 1933. Their ostentatious company name was displayed outside and a 3-manual 7-unit Compton added to the amenities. This was notable in that the console was mounted on a turn-table platform-lift. Reginald New inaugurated the instrument on the 25 February 1934.

Once again, ABC inherited from Union, and renamed the Majestic the ABC in 1965. The organ had been kept playable, so went first to a private house in Keighley during 1969, then on to a social club in West Hallam. From Boxing Day 1972, the ABC became a triple in the usual manner. The balcony is no. 1, down from 755 to 576 seats and there are 320 and 107 seats respectively in screens 2 and 3. Some curtaining and dark blue decor conceal the original shape and form of the auditorium, but the general appearance is pleasing. Screen 1 retains its mahogany entrance surround, and staff have removed some insensitive paintwork from the marble banisters. Hopefully, as the only cinema in north-west Kent, Cannon will keep the flag flying in Gravesend.

NORTHFLEET, only 3 miles from Gravesend, nevertheless maintained its own cinema for 45 years. The original building was first listed in a 1912/13 directory, standing halfway down the High Street and backing on to a chalk pit. Being a close knit community, the cinema contented itself with advertising through billboards and handbills, until the lure of Gravesend caused a change of policy in January 1916. Yet in only a month, *Gravesend Reporter* publicity carried an announcement of closure. This was to allow reinforcement of the foundations due to subsidence into the chalk pit. This done, business resumed. Talkies renewed interest sufficiently to lead UDC Chairman Jessie Clements to build a new cinema next to the old one, which closed with 'The Three Kings' on the 27 December 1929. Here a new sheet metal floor was laid to withstand the skaters who were to throng the Astoria Dance Salon from the 4 April 1931. The balcony became an observation lounge overlooking couples dancing to Jack Lane and his Band. In wartime, the **Astoria** served as a public hall, whose varied uses included wedding receptions.

The New Astoria opened the day after the old cinema went dark, and was leased by Mr Clements to Lion Cinematograph Co, Whitcombe Street, London. Appraised of the chalk pit menace, architects F. W. Wilkins and G. G. Winborne had this cinema built side on to the main street. Quickly the name Astoria changed to Strathcona by 1938, to Star in September 1940 and shortly afterwards to **Wardona**. Not an original Wardona, it was the only cinema in this circuit with BT-H sound and boasted the cheapest seat prices. Next door, the dance hall retained the Astoria name and became the home of the locally famed Marjory Shades dancing school, which outlived the cinema by a year or two. The Wardona cinema closed on the 1 December 1957 blaming that chalk pit again. Both buildings have now vanished, a petrol station now roughly marking the site, with Blue Circle owning land to the rear. Lacking anything more tangible, the sound of the Glen Miller orchestra playing 'In The Mood' is enough for one lady. This was invariably played at the Wardona to calm the audience who endured not infrequent breaks in the programme due to 'operating difficulties' in the box.

The Plaza, Gravesend, in Union Cinema days (CTA)

Maidstone's Pavilion (renamed Ritz in 1935), c.1937 (Les Bull)

The auditorium of Maidstone Granada, showing Christie organ

MAIDSTONE

Much of cinema interest in the county town has been swept away by commercial pressures, although **MAIDSTONE** does have one of the few Granadas still showing films. Eight decades ago, the first flickers or 'bio tableaux' were seen in Transfield's Hippodrome – just before it closed. This was in 1904, the year also of the first children's bioscope shows at the Corn Exchange. Regular adult shows followed in 1905, given by such travelling entrepreneurs as North American Illuminated Pictures and St Louis Pictures. A major advance came in February 1910 when on the 16th, the **Empire Electric Theatre** opened opposite the East Station. Empire Electric Theatres offered two 105 minute shows at 7 and 9 p.m. A sample might be 'The Diver' – a thrilling story of love and hatred and attempted murder at the bottom of the sea, and rescue by a submarine. All was not well on land however, for a prospectus appeared in the press during August 1910 for a new cinema. The older hall disclaimed any connection with the Maidstone Electric Theatre Ltd enterprise, but was forced out of business by the advent of a purpose-built cinema. This arose at 17 Earl Street, employing county architects Ruck and Smith in the design work. It opened on the 15 February 1911 and was to seat 450 in a hall measuring 100 by 30-ft.

A conversion job followed swiftly on the Electric, when the old Maidstone Pavilion Skating Rink turned to pictures on the 18 March. Skating had begun in Pudding Lane during September 1909, but had palled. Pictures were the obvious remedy. We meet the Popular Picture Palace Co. again giving twice nightly shows and 'star' programmes to pull the crowds. Manager Leslie Derby gave 2/6d to anyone able to spot himself on the screen after a local filming. The PPP prospered and was taken over in December 1919 by F. T. Wiggins, who enlarged both screen and stage, redecorated, replaced projection equipment and brought seating capacity up to 1,350. Next year, he installed Automaticket machines to speed the queues. Somehow, another 100 were seated to watch the popular 'two star films'. The floor was raked by now, but the girders of the old skating rink stayed until a £4,000 conversion hid them above a new asbestos ceiling. The £4,000 also paid for new embossed velvet seating, a perforated white rubber Westone screen and Western Electric sound – all without closing.

The press sympathised with the fate of the displaced tenants of Bonny's Yard who were forced to move out to make way for the **Central** cinema in King Street. This was again designed by Ruck and Smith for a local company whose managing director was J. H. Kent. When opened on the 7 February 1921, the granite and masonry frontage with third floor faced in old English timber was incomplete, but the 1,250 seat auditorium had been distempered in cream and buff. There was a moulded ceiling and triple globes hanging from the pilasters, the centre ones giving out a low blue light during the films. The first one of these was 'Alf's Button' supplemented by a 7-piece orchestra and a 3-manual straight organ. The organ pipes were in a loft to the left of the proscenium. All Central employees were ex military men, used to putting in a smart appearance. A tea room overlooking King Street opened 6 months later where an orchestra entered for a 90 minute tea time slot.

The 8th wonder of the world (sic), came to the Central when De Forest's sound on disc phonograph films played here, namely comedy or music shorts with elaborately synchronised sound. More superlatives greeted the talkie 'The Jazz Singer' in April 1929 and the all talking 'House Of Secrets' that September. The Central found its way to the ABC circuit by way of Messrs Overland and Benjamin (1930) and Union Cinemas (1935). In wartime, 1,000 children responded to appeals for waste paper – free matinee tickets were given to any child bringing in 5lbs or more. What war failed to do came to pass on the 27 June 1955, when the Central was severely damaged by fire. Firemen bravely stood in the blazing balcony until it collapsed. Ironically, a £10,000 screen had just been installed. As we shall see, this was the second ABC house to succumb to fire within 17 months, so a new cinema arose here from the ashes.

The builders engaged in 1921, G. E. Wallis & Sons came back in 1956 to resurrect their handiwork. ABC architects C. J. Foster and R. J. Westway supervised the project, and presumably were also involved in the removal of the proscenium arch before the fire, to accommodate a new 38-ft cinemascope screen. Now the integral shop fronts were swept away, and glazed timber doors and a new canopy with glass fascia replaced them. Recessed downlights lit the pavement and the new name (**Ritz**) blazed in neon from the fin. Inside, a double staircase led to the 401 seat balcony or down to the 869 stalls seats. These were protected from street noise by 2 sets of double doors. The auditorium was roomy and decoratively restrained. Improved oil-fired central heating, better air conditioning and RCA sound were refinements made possible by the rebuilding. Despite its simplicity, the new Ritz possessed cinema atmosphere with its comfortable red worsted velvet seating and mushroom-coloured satin festoon curtain. Re-opening took place with 'Moby Dick' on the 10 December 1956. The Ritz was the last ABC house in Maidstone to show films, being renamed the **ABC** in 1962. However, bingo players were ill served, and the Granada conversion was yet to come. Hence the ABC closed with 'Legend Of The Seven Golden Vampires' on the 5 October, 1974. Francis Young, the chief projectionist and son of Frederick Young, who managed the Central, had hoped for a circle only cinema, but Mecca took sole possession. Bingo too proved insupportable after the Granada club had creamed off many of the players. Hence the ABC came down in the late seventies to make way for a branch of Boots the chemist.

The **Palace Theatre**, Gabriels Hill (1908) had included Palascope (sic) films in the programming early on to supplement variety. The Palace held 1,200 and was altered in 1920 so that the gallery ran through to the boxes. Messrs Overland and Benjamin bought the Palace in 1930 hoping to put on straight theatre. Maidstone could not support such a venture, so the auditorium was redecorated and reseated and a Westone screen erected, on which 'All Quiet On The Western Front' was shown. The Palace closed in June 1935, but was back from 3 October as a Union Cinemas house. As their third Maidstone outlet, the Palace had a chequered life. For a time (spring, 1948 to April 1952) only stage shows were presented. Films returned, but were only given a financial boost by the Central fire in June 1955. ABC had recently allowed film shows to lapse but revived them in the Palace from the 18 July 1955 until their new Ritz was well established. After films finally ceased to run in the old theatre after the 19 October 1957, the building was demolished to make way for a branch of Sainsburys. This later became a Robert Dyas shop.

We mentioned 3 Union acquisitions. Third in sequence but not in importance to the circuit was the **Pavilion**, Pudding Lane. Already refurbished ready for sound, Union made further alterations after taking over on the 5 October 1935, i.e. a new façade, fresh seats, refurbished foyer and a 3-manual 6-unit Compton organ. This chimed 8 p.m. on the opening night, following which the curtains parted to reveal the mayor, Alderman Tyrwhitt-Drake on stage. The chosen film, 'Heart's Desire' was screened, followed by Leonora Corbett live on stage plus Bobby Howell's Broadcasting Band. The new owners claimed that the former 'garish' colour scheme had been banished and a new elaborate stage and dressing rooms added. All this revitalising merited the renaming of the cinema as the **Ritz**, a name not to be confused with Maidstone's postwar Ritz already mentioned. The reuse of the name is explained by the disastrous fire which took hold on the night of 11 January 1954. Forty firemen fought the blaze, which woke up half the town, but 1,421 cinema seats were taken off Maidstone's tally that night. The Central took over bookings until it too had its inferno. Was not ABC unlucky in losing two cinemas in one town so quickly! This Ritz disappeared to make way for shops and offices known as Cornwallis House. Today another Ritz has followed the first one into oblivion.

What of the old Electric in Earl Street? This was renamed The Medina c.1938 and acquired by Mr and Mrs Charles Senior. They completely redecorated and refurbished the cinema, rebuilt the proscenium for a wider screen, and British Talking Pictures provided a new sound system. As usual, improvements merited a name change – to **Regal**. Despite many changes, the American style paybox and old-fashioned external look of the place lived on until closure. Still independent with a capacity down to 318, the Regal finally closed on the 18 March 1957. A Trustee Savings bank arose on the site.

Today's cinemagoers are left with a much altered **Granada** in Lower Stone Street. This massive brick building facing the bus station has a stone-pillared cornerpiece facing uphill, and characteristic Granada style windows along the side elevation. Built on the site of Tomlin's furniture stores, the Granada was the work of Cecil Massey in conjunction with the famed designer, Komisarjevsky. With 1,800 seats, it was Maidstone's largest, and included a café over the main entrance. Prior to severe modernisation, the interior had the look still largely visible in Granadas in Bedford, Harrow etc. At the opening on the 10 January 1934, a 3-manual 8-unit Christie organ completed the picture, being inaugurated by Alex Taylor, who stayed for 4 months. The installation included a full size Steck grand piano on stage, playable from the organ console.

41

The scale of operations needed in a big pre-war cinema can be deduced from publicity collated for the third anniversary in 1937. By then, the café had served 143,686 eggs, 2,233,546 patrons had eaten 76 tons of ice cream, been given 76 miles of tickets, seen 4,278 miles of British film and heard 41,080 melodies on the organ. Fifteen thousand of these carefully documented patrons came to consume a ¾-ton anniversary cake, baked by F. A. Smith & Son. By then staff who welcomed them had earned £14,316 in wages and 9 page boys had outgrown their uniforms! In wartime, a 'saloon bar' was added, but not for drinks – it was a booth to sell war savings certificates put up when the film 'Saloon Bar' was being shown.

By diversifying into bingo, Granada began to change their main business. Here, the architects George Cole & Partners and the circuit's own building design unit executed a conversion which isolated the stalls area for bingo, and created a 560-cinema above and a mini 90-seater in the old café, already closed. Patrons now entered the cinemas from a new side entrance, with street level paybox, ascending to a first floor lounge and sales area. Bingo enthusiasts enter through the original doors, their domain now carpeted in green with white wall curtaining. Little of the original Komisarjevsky decor now survives. Some murals went to head office. In December 1974, the main cinema was split into two, so that Granadas 1 and 3 now seat 258 and 259 apiece. These have a sombre dark chocolate decor with orange curtaining covering the screen and surrounding area. Down Rotaflex lighting is used and the projection is now provided by 2 Italian Cinemeccania machines capable of handling 6,000-ft of film. The intention of Granada was to develop cinema and bingo equally, but this approach has not been repeated elsewhere. The Christie was extensively damaged by floodwater in September 1968. Minus the irreparable console, the instrument was shipped out to Australia for the Queensland Theatre Organ Society. These stalwarts installed it in Kelvin Grove State High School.

Before leaving Maidstone, we should note that it was here that the first drive-in movies came to the Kent Garden Centre in April 1984. Drive-in Movie (UK) provided space for 150 cars to park in front of a portable screen. Family films were shown 5 nights a week, with American style waitresses serving hamburgers. The venture did not resume in 1985 – are the British unreceptive to drive-ins? A much earlier open-air cinema had been tried in the Zoological Gardens, Tovil back in 1914, but was closed on the outbreak of war. The Guinness Book of Records futher recalls that Maidstone Gaol held the earliest recorded film shows for prisoners. This was in the gaol chapel which held 100. From November 1937, inmates of good conduct could watch the pictures, which were brought to them by projectionists who were 'lifers'.

MEDWAY TOWNS

Cinemas retreated from west of the river first, but today, there is just one Cannon left to boom out the big screen message for the entire conurbation. Earliest on the **STROOD** scene was Solly Goodman's **Gem**, 3–4 Station Road. Built by T. Cornelius & Co. (Gillingham), it opened on Christmas Eve, 1910. This followed on from Goodman Entertainment Co.'s earlier Gem in Gillingham. Billed as 'the most comfortable hall in Kent' but one lady recalls having to perch on the edge of her seat to avoid sagging springs! Some years before the advent of the 'X' certificate, the Gem showed one film from which all under 16 were excluded, namely 'White Slave Traffic' cleared for an exclusive run by the National Council of Morals. Around 1932, the Gem passed to Jessie Slight, who renamed it Queens. He in turn leased the cinema to Herbert Grose, who put on a new front and ran two other cinemas in Snodland and Queenborough from here. By this time (1935), the box was equipped with projectors from A. W. Harris, of Moreton-in-Marsh. This box was where the lessees spent the night during a major flood! Children flocked to the 2d rush, and as the toilets were outside, additional ones returned! Altogether about 700 legitimate patrons could be seated. After war broke out, films ceased, but in April 1941, the Queens was advertising variety. This too lost out to competition, and the building fell heir to varied light industrial uses, the last known being a crash repair and windscreen fitting service.

The rival **Kings Picture Palace**, 1–3 London Road, had only 300 seats and some say it was a fleapit. A 2-storey brick store was gutted, and entrance foyer with paybox added at the east end, and a concrete and Uralite projection box added. The uralite came from the Higham works. This hall was opened by Coronation Cinematograph Co. on the 15 April 1911. Outclassed by Strood's third cinema, the Kings closed in 1922, thereafter passing to Strood Motor and Engineering Co. The building stayed with the motor trade almost until demolition in 1978. One side wall with carved stone decorations lasted until 1984. A petrol station now marks the site facing Gun Lane.

Croneen's final Medway town **Invicta** saw off the Kings. Erected in the High Street, this 600-seater opened on the 19 November 1919. It was equipped with Bland projectors and had a 22 by 18-ft screen. However, the Croneens disposed of this Invicta to Stanley Hinds of Walthamstow, when their Plaza, Gillingham was being built. Closed in 1945 by bomb damage, the cinema was restored by Oliver Ward and reopened in January 1947 as a Wardona. As such it remained until the 26 January 1958, thereafter being replaced by a Shoppers Paradise supermarket. A fourth cinema planned for the town by Union Cinemas in 1937 was aborted due to that company's financial difficulties.

ROCHESTER saw films a little ahead of Strood, having the **Corn Exchange** (1706) to utilise. The Royal Canadian Picture Co. used the Exchange from the 10 October 1910. Patrons in velvet and red leather tip-up seats were shown one of the first maritime dramas ever filmed – 'Stars And Stripes'. Films ran until 1924, after which there appears to be an intriguing gap. Remodelled internally in 1961, the Corn Exchange is still easily found next to Rochester Library.

The gap looked like being filled when on the 5 May 1933, the local press revealed that the city was to get Kent's largest cinema. It would cost £75,000, complete with dance hall, café and roof garden, and was to be called the Astoria. Plans and name were changed as the consortium responsible, Southern Proprietory Holdings worked on the project. The managing director was David Weston, brother of Harry, the cinema architect, but Arthur Kenyon designed the new Majestic. Small shops opposite the county court gave way to the High Street super cinema, which opened on the 15 April 1935, to a triumphant fanfare from the Royal Marines. Ralph Lynn was guest of honour. A 3-manual 11-unit Compton with lift and solo cello attachment burst into life at the touch of J. W. Hartland, who prefaced the opening films – 'Million Dollar Ransom' and 'The Iron Duke'. Rather massive externally, the **Majestic** was more intimate within, using concealed lighting. Two thousand one hundred and eighty-one could be seated, 783 of these in the balcony. A pot of tea with matching milk jug would be passed round the rear stalls during the matinees. There was also a delightful café seating 50, and dance hall. After this closed in October 1957 by the way, it became Rank's 15th Victor Sylvester dance studio from the following February.

Although managed from the outset by Gaumont British, a distinctive title logo incorporating the city arms was used in press advertising. Sadly some Dickensian motifs, planned for the foyer never materialised. The Majestic handled its own publicity, hiring a man to drive round distributing playbills in a new Morris Minor van. Jack Hartland left after 6 months, and Lew Harris and Clarence Barber followed as organists. Chatham-born George Blackmore was appointed resident organist in May 1939, although only 18 then. From May 1941, he broadcast the Majestic sound, even when serving in the RAF. Less famous was the Saturday morning children's organist, Uncle Clem Waghorn, whose audience were hardest to please of all. He soon had them singing lustily, shouting, whistling etc. Clem scratched the song's words one-eighth of an inch high on to slides which magnified to a foot high on screen. Clem left his 2,000 club members in 1946, moving on to Seabrook.

Gaumont bought the freehold, and changed the name to **Gaumont** from the 3 April 1950. Apart from a charity concert in 1953, the big stage did not really come alive until the Cyril Stapleton Bandshow was booked on the 1 October 1957. Big names followed on for a decade, the Rolling Stones for example invoking a cauldron of hysteria in May 1965. In 1967, 70mm and 6-track stereo came to the cinema, and was soon used to advantage in an 8-week run of 'The Sound Of Music'. Other postwar highlights included the sale of the organ in 1961 to an Orpington church – it is now in the Civic Hall, Middelburg, however. The Gaumont became the **Odeon** from the 21 October 1962, and lastly Rank tripled the cinema from March 1974. There was now a 700 circle no. 1 plus 2 120-seat minis. The re-opening was one of the last ceremonies performed by the old style mayor of Rochester. However, the Odeon was not ideally sited to serve the

Medway towns with Rank programming and sadly joined the group to close on the 31 October 1981. Bingo had been considered ever since 1970, but after years of dereliction, the go-ahead for 55 replacement old peoples flats finally came in December 1986.

Due north of Rochester, the village of **CLIFFE-AT-HOO** adapted an old government building into their cinema during 1921. The now vanished **Globe** stood in Church Street north of the Higham/Cooling Road intersection, west side. The Globe was ready for August Bank Holiday (then 1 August), when 'Ivanhoe' was shown. This 300 seat hall was run in turn by Messrs Edwin Thompson, J. Hollamby and R. G. Whitaker. As soon as the lights dimmed, children flitted from the cheaper seats into the dearer ones! Date of closure for the ex-(cinema) directory cinema is uncertain, but it was up for sale late in 1965 and quickly demolished. A row of 5 terraced houses mark the site today.

CHATHAM being the hub of much of the entertainment in the area, it was quick to welcome the bioscope. A machine was placed in the gallery of Barnard's Palace of Varieties (1886) at 107–111 High Street. An extra 'turn' was also brought to the Gaiety Music Hall (1890–1911) in the form of an Edisonograph. Both were whirring by January 1910. Barnards lasted until destroyed by fire in 1934, and the Gaiety was replaced by the Empire on the same site. A converted shop at 74 High Street became the 'silent drama home of Chatham – the real home of the picture world'. This real home was the **Cinema de Luxe**, opened on the 22 January 1910. Children and ladies were especially welcome, but the long wooden benches were not quite 'de Luxe'. However, you could bring your own cushion! Suffragettes were dimly regarded in the first film, 'Scroggins Puts Up for Blankshire'. The De Luxe was renamed the Silver and from 1921, the Corner House. As the name implies, this 'dainty up-to-date bijou house' had a café, a sunny room painted lemon-yellow with blue curtains. Customers sat at oak tables with snowy table cloths and lemon lampshades. They could order food or writing paper – yellow of course. Waitresses wore blue frocks and muslin caps and aprons. Sadly the Corner House closed in 1922. Subsequently the premises became a gas showrooms and latterly have been offices for H.F.C. Trust Ltd.

Next year, 1911, a purpose-built cinema came to Chatham. 205 High Street was the site for **National Electric Theatres** to augment their chain of halls, which already existed in Leeds, Halifax and Burton-on-Trent. Melville Ward was employed to design a 38 by 100-ft hall seating 639. The front was rendered in Exelstone plaster (stone imitation) which was illuminated after dark. A 20-ft square vestibule with paybox led into a dark oak and peacock blue auditorium with a small balcony. On the first night (15 April) the films were out of focus, but the National Electric persevered. On the 4 October 1928, a fire broke out in the box . . . but the orchestra played on. Curiously, the film 'Fire' had played the week before, and was reputed to have caused a fire everywhere it played. Denman Picture Houses acquired the National in the early thirties. This was a subsidiary of Gaumont British, who had outlets in the Majestic, Rochester and Palace, Chatham. Thus the older cinema became a second-run house with peeling paint. It finally closed on the 24 February 1951 showing two immortals – 'Magnificent Brute' and Abbott and Costello in 'On The Carpet'. In the aftermath, Wilson's Fashion store were in residence until September 1983, and they kept the raked floor. Now, Best Sellers retail here.

Just visible up a passage beside Woolworths, in Fullager's Yard, was the old **Invicta** cinema. This was the Croneen's second Invicta – we have met the third one in Strood. The Invicta opened on the 7 February 1916 and stayed with Croneen until disposed of to J. H. Canvin in April 1929. Films lasted until 1939. Thereafter the Invicta was used by the Church Army and, postwar, became a warehouse. In 1962, Gerry Cameron spent £20,000 altering the building from an ailing indoor market into an entertainment centre. Fittings from the defunct Empire were used to fit out the back bar, and ballroom dancing, wrestling and bingo were offered. The music became more frantic and the Rolling Stones were here in March 1964. Bingo was in the ascendant and the Gaming Bord favoured exclusive dedication to the game. Mrs Cameron sold the club to Coral to raise capital and it remained with them until closed in March 1985. Bass-Charrington acquired the Thorn-EMI clubs for its subsidiary, Coral in 1983. These included the Chatham Ritz, into which Coral are now concentrated. The surplus Invicta was awaiting some alternative, possibly leisure use at time of writing.

Still on the High Street, yet another cinema opened at no. 49. This was the **Picture House**, adjacent to the Chatham Empire. Purpose designed by the Rochester architect, H. H. Dunstall, capacity here confidently went up to 1,100. An approach along the theatre's west side led to a square vestibule with painted glass roof, and beyond, an auditorium flanked by ionic pilasters and capitals of 'chaste design'. There was a circular ceiling and fine entablature consisting of enriched cornice, architraves and frieze. The pipes of an orchestra organ flanked both sides of the screen. The 2-manual Nicholson and Lord console, with stopkeys instead of drawstops, was sited in the orchestra pit. The screen was given a bronze surround to achieve that art gallery look then in vogue. The new cinema was jointly managed by theatre magnate Oswald Stoll and Alderman H. E. Davis.

The Picture House opened on the 19 February 1917, showing proudly our new weapon in 'Advance Of The Tanks'. Harry Davidson of Old Tyme Dancing fame, and H. Nicholson from the organ firm were at the console. 'Chatham's palatial cinema' booked some popular hits. 'Why do you torture me like this?' entreated the girl of Rudolph Valentino on the 1926 poster for 'Son Of The Sheik'. The Picture House ran in tandem with the Empire but in the thirties turned downmarket, booking low budget westerns from the Republic and Monogram studios. In the forties, Mancunian Film Corporation comedies like those made by Norman Evans and Frank Randle found a home here. Cheap horror or sci-fi films followed in vogue, of the genre 'Earth Versus Flying Saucers'. Greatly daring, a Harrison Marks nude travelogue – 'Around The World With Nothing On' played on the 19 April 1959. The name of the cinema had changed to **Empire** from the 1 February 1953, but even Marks' feast of beauty, colour and interest

46

The Majestic (later Gaumont) Rochester, in 1935 (Les Bull)

The sumptuous interior of the Chatham Empire, c. 1930 (Doris Wilkins)

failed to revive the flagging Empire. Outlasting big brother by a year, it closed down with 'Doctor In Love' and 'Congo Crossing' on the 10 June 1961. The whole site became a car park, on part of which Anchorage House now stands.

Next door, the **Chatham Empire** (Frank Matcham, 1912) rose in place of the Gaiety. Messrs Stoll and Davis were again in partnership. The former formed 12 of his theatres into a cinema circuit during 1929, and this one had a projection box jutting out on to the balcony. It was equipped with both Vitaphone sound on disc from Warner and the Fox Movietone sound on film apparatus. The less reliable Vitaphone nevertheless gave Chatham the famed film, 'The Singing Fool' which ran from the 15 July 1929, 5 times daily for a month, with successive supporting features. The concurrent advent of RCA sound at the Ritz was completely overshadowed. Films remained a key part of the entertainment, so much so that the orchestra pit was covered over. Films helped to sustain the Empire, especially when the Theatre Royal was closed by fire in 1937/38. A two-week run of 'Victoria The Great' was booked to mark this opportunity.

By Stoll's death in 1942, his theatres were in receivership, and the Empire was dark for 20 months. Re-opened by Prince Littler in April 1942, a 'live only' policy prevailed, the stage being re-equipped for that end. Sold after the war to the People's Entertainment Society (a group of Cooperative societies), the Empire struggled on with various lessees, the final one trying out a cabaret dining policy a la 'Talk of the Town'. With power unbendingly cut off after an unpaid account, the Empire closed impecuniously on the 31 March 1960 and was bought by Chatham Town Council for redevelopment.

The elegant Theatre Royal, 102 High Street (George Bond, 1900), was a legitimate theatre built for Charles and Lionel Barnard. This too turned to the silver screen as 'Kent's latest super (Western Electric) talkie theatre'. William Robinson of Brighton bankrupted himself to show 'What A Widow' and more during 1931/32. The next proprietor opted for big name variety stars like Max Miller and Harry Lauder. Andrew Mather modernised the interior, after the stage area was destroyed by fire in December 1937. Later lessees of the People's Entertainment Society changed the name to Royal Hippodrome and back to Theatre Royal – twice – but the lights went out on the 20 May 1955. More on the theatre can be read in the 'Curtains' theatres directory, published in 1982.

Unlike the Cannon, the old **Imperial Picture Palace** was built end on to the street. The original 1914 building was of red brick with stone dressings in the 'free Renaissance style'. Like the Theatre Royal it was the work of George Bond, costing altogether £11,000. The well isolated box had a 100-ft throw to the 18½ by 14½-ft screen. The capacity was high for that time at 1,674, and amenities included the IPP Ladies Orchestra, under the direction of Miss Brewin. 'You may come in at any time and see the pictures round' promised the Imperial. 'Pictures are here to stay' proclaimed the mayor, G. F. Butts at the opening on the 28 January (cheers). The IPP was acquired by W. W. Thompson of the Grand, Gillingham on the 29 August 1927 and rechristened the **New Regent**. ABC took control early in 1929, and had installed a 2-manual 8-unit Christie organ in time for Easter Monday. Charles Willis came from the Queens, Forest Gate to play the opening chords. Some variety was put on until talkies began to play from the 15 July 1929. Increased business merited a two-week closure for renovation and new seating during June 1931.

A complete rebuilding followed in 1937 under the direction of W. R. Glen. A massive brick elevation, relieved by faience framing of windows and roof line, took shape in time for a low-key start on the 11 July 1938. A civic party attended a matinee show of 'Housemaster' starring Otto Kruger and Diana Churchill, and then crossed over to the Ritz café, where they heard that ABC were then issuing no less than 200 million tickets a year. Back at the Regent, a typical Glen interior, elegant and functional, had been decorated in shades of pink and blue, merging into brown on the side walls. Seating was now 1,906 (755 in the circle). The stage curtains of silk had butterfly and floral patterns on a gold background. A new Compton organ had been considered, but the chambers remained empty – ABC had an organ at their newly acquired Ritz nearby. The sound equipment was RCA, later Perspecta, a forerunner of stereo. Simplex projectors in turn gave way to Ross GC3s and then Phillips FP 20s. These, now adapted to non-rewind, remain in situ in the blue-tiled and parquet-floored projection room.

As the ABC, the cinema closed for tripling in January 1972. The single 1,647 seat auditorium became three, holding 528, 366 and 172 to cope with the entire conurbation. After Arthur Allen succeeded George Williams as manager, a small cinema heritage exhibition was placed in unused space up the main staircase, during 1979. A map of by-gone Medway town cinemas, photographs, a bench seat from the Gem, Faversham etc. are preserved. ABC seats which survived several floods and a major fire under the circle in January 1962, have found their way to the Medway Little Theatre, Rochester. In 1986, this and other ABCs became part of the **Cannon** circuit.

Over the road, the sumptuous **Ritz** was built on the site of Axe brand's clothing factory. This was once the Chatham Union workhouse, a curious link with the Ritz's mentors, Union Cinemas. Externally, Robert Cromie's Ritz was lit by floodlights and supported two large Ritz signs to attract road and rail users – they still remain today. The 2,322 seat cinema opened with unprecedented ballyhoo. Actor, Jack Buchanan was mobbed by his fans as he arrived to offi-ciate. Also there were the Billy Cotton Band, the Dagenham Girl Pipers and Harold Ramsay at the 3-manual 8-unit Wurlitzer. Ramsay was Union's controller of entertainment and he designed the organ, which was equipped with a second lift for a piano attachment. A mock version of radio's 'In Town Tonight' was played out by local celebrities and the audience settled down to watch 'My Man Godfrey'. A GPO landline linked this Ritz with another being opened in Barnsley, also on the 22 March 1937. Only a fire at the Crystal Palace upstaged the ceremony, but days later the management showered a local baby born nearest the day with gifts and a life pass to the cinema – where are you now, Margaret Ann Batchelor?

Technically, the high fidelity Mirrorphonic sound won praise, as surely did the

Kent's largest cinema, the 2,322 seat Ritz, Chatham (Tony Turner)

splendid chandeliered restaurant. This was open until midnight, 7 days a week, although fuel shortages ended Sunday openings during 1947. The Ritz had a large stage suited for cine-variety, which began on 5 April. However, they ceased when ABC acquired the ailing Union chain, but not before Stainless Stephen, the comedian who 'spoke' his punctuation, came on the 5 September. Wurlitzer sounds could be heard until the mid-fifties, when the stage made a come-back. Peter Brough of 'Educating Archie' fame came to town in April 1954 and 'Britain's dynamic teenage idol' Tommy Steele, in September 1957. Although equipped with a new sound system in 1964, the various one-night stands by the Batchelors, the Yardbirds and even David Frost failed to break even. Undaunted, ABC brought in Phillips DP 70 projection, which gave Chatham 'Doctor Zhivago' in 70mm, '2001, A Space Odyssey' and a two-part production of 'War And Peace' followed on, but the public were not to be pleased. Plans for bingo were confirmed in October 1971. A steamy double bill – 'Naked Countess' and 'I Do It My Way' closed cinema at the Ritz on the 20 May 1972. Leased to the Leeds based Star Group, bingo began with minimum delay. EMI ran the club themselves from 1975–83, but Corals inherited the club, already expensively refurbished during 1978. The organ was removed in 1972.

Uphill towards Gillingham, Gaumont British acquired a controlling interest in Palace (Gillingham) Ltd, then building a cinema in Watling Street. The site, just inside Chatham, enabled the cinema to take advantage of that borough's more liberal Sunday opening rules. Gillingham forbade cinemas to open until after Sunday services for all the period up to the last war. Cliffords, a local builders, leased the land at an advantageous rate, as a cinema would make a welcome contribution to a developing area. Sister to the earlier Majestic, Rochester, the **Palace** opened on the 30 November 1936. Smaller in size but still large at a 1,864 capacity, the cinema was designed by W. Kenyon at a cost of £50,000. This included a large café/dance hall with 4 large windows running from floor to ceiling. Key external features were the 280-ft canopy and the commanding clock tower, which used a scarlet coronet and multi-coloured neon to arrest passers-by. A 3-manual 7-unit Compton, with lift, played inside.

This suburban super, although most comfortable, never enjoyed very good business. Patrons were tempted by a car park, opposite the entrance, and during 1937/38, Sunday band shows were added whilst the Theatre Royal was closed. Talent shows ran for much longer. After being opened by Terence Casey, the organ was to respond to the touch of Peter Kilbey and the local methodist church organist, Fred Ralph. The Palace became the **Gaumont** from the 18 December 1950. Although mainly showing films concurrently with the Rochester Gaumont, this one suffered a slow death, closing ultimately with 'The Captain's Table' on the 2 February 1961. Rank spent £250,000 converting the interior into a 24-lane Top Rank Bowl, opened appropriately on the 18 December 1961 by a descendant of Sir Francis Drake. Bowls faded in popularity, but this was the last Top Rank Bowl to close – on the 31 October 1970. A B&Q store and latterly a camping centre occupy the old cinema, but the interior is completely gutted – even the main staircase is not original. The organ was scrapped in 1961.

A non-public cinema existed in **HMS Pembroke** (naval barracks) at the far end away from the main entrance. Brick built, it held under 500 and had a slight rake down to the proscenium arch and stage. Doubling as a venue for live shows, pantomimes and lectures, it was run by Mr Simmonds, the welfare secretary. It survived long enough to be equipped for cinemascope, but date of closure is unknown.

GILLINGHAM's Hippodrome theatre showed a series of films as early as October 1906. The building stood where Balmoral Gardens is now, but was converted into a skating rink in 1909 and demolished in 1921. A former mineral water plant at 13/17 King Street was acquired by Solly Goodman, then a concert party promoter, to present Goodman's variety and bioscope entertainment. The adapted hall opened on the 19 January 1910 with 'the most wonderful pictures ever seen' e.g. 'Nero And The Burning Of Rome'. First named the Victoria Hall and then the **Gem**, cine variety was presented twice nightly plus two matinees, and sacred concerts were held on Sundays. The newly-opened Grand spurred a further upgrading of the Gem in 1911. It reopened on the 13 November, having been redecorated by D. Gilardoni in white enamel with red wallpaper on the upper halves of the walls. Fake marble statues, ferns and a raked floor completed the transformation. Bertram Garrett, then only aged 25, took over in 1928, and he installed a Panotrope to accompany the silent pictures. The Gem was soon renamed the Kings Hall Talkie Cinema, but was closed by a serious fire on the 17 June 1935. Cinema never returned, but the shell housed a garage and then a timber store, the rather dilapidated canopy still visible. On film tastes, Mr Garrett once pronounced: 'The love stuff always goes, but people like a real spectacular now and then, like "The Ten Commandments"'.

The **Grand** opened in late 1910 (26 November), and was also a cine variety house. Built on the corner of Skinner and Jeffery Streets, the huge gilt dome over the entrance was still incomplete. The architect, Ewan Barr is better known for the Duchess Theatre, London, and some Astoria interiors. Here the 800 seat semi classical auditorium innovatively provided the best sight lines from the rear of the hall. There was close carpeting even in the cheaper parts of the house. There were two boxes at the back of the circle and a spacious buffet. Programming included live acts, for example the noted Lady Little, only 13½ inches tall, and Leoni Clark, the cat king, who had trained 200 cats, dogs, mice, monkeys and canaries to do his bidding. After a fortnight's closure, the Grand reopened on the 6 April 1914, purely as a cinema. This popular venue had several proprietors including W. W. Thompson of the Regent, Chatham, Eric Rhodes (later managing director of Classic Cinemas), and from 1949, Stan and Keith Darrell. The brothers carried out a redecoration and later installed cinemascope. Outstanding 'art' films were booked, – 'The Cranes Are Flying' or 'Bread, Love And Dreams'. The children were encouraged with a price cut to 6d. Such enterprise failed in the end, for the Grand closed with 'Duel At Silver Creek' and 'Behemoth The Sea Monster' on the 12 November 1960. Punitive entertainment tax and TV were to blame. Demolished in 1965, a filling station was built on the site, and itself replaced by a tyre depot. A figure of Venus from the dome survives in a Gillingham garden, the dome and canopy, incidentally, having been taken down in December 1957, predeceasing the cinema itself.

The Croneen family are associated with their Invictas. William was landlord of the original Lord Hardinge pub and his son Horace ran a silversmiths next door. Horace moved further along to make room for a cinema to be built between High and Mill Streets. One hundred people were turned away when their first **Invicta** cinema opened up on the 13 April 1914. However, the occasion was low key – Mabel Payne sang the National Anthem at this 'home of instruction and amusement'. A framed plaster screen was called 'a big improvement on the usual sheet'. Bricks from their own brickworks were used by architect E. J. Hammond in the construction. Thirty light bulbs surrounded a rampant invicta, flanked by statues holding red globes in sundry niches. There was a 10 by 12-ft entrance hall leading to a 500 seat main floor or 100 seat balcony. Harry Bennett, a local decorator, had painted a night sky effect on the ceiling.

From the opening film, 'Truth Will Out' the Invicta played on until the talkies prompted the Croneens to contemplate a new cinema. The Invicta closed on the 11 July 1931, but by next Easter was back as the short-lived Coliseum theatre. Rep and touring novelty acts were brought to Gillingham by various lessees, but after September 1933 the theatre became the Invicta Garage. The building stayed intact, but after 1968, the auditorium was only used for storage and thus deteriorated. D.O.E. offices now mark the site.

An unsuccessful cinema opened at 93 Pier Road in an old Baptist mission chapel. Run by Messrs H. R. Richardson and William Friday, the **Pier Road** cinema was plagued by constant breakdowns and only existed between 1922 and 1924.

Disposing of their 3 Invictas, the Croneens (in this case Walter and his brother Horace), embarked on their **Plaza** in Duncan Road. E. J. Hammond was re-engaged, but the front was the work of Barnards of Maidstone. Notable features included the elegant wrought ironwork of the staircase panelling, and the fine iron and glass canopy, both the work of Courtfield Engineering. The four columns supporting the canopy came from supports used on the tramway system closed the year before! The Plaza was innovative, installing Blackheat electric tubular heaters under most seating. During the heating season, the copper components ticked eerily as they expanded. Up in the box, a rarely seen lady projectionist, Miss Barnes, had been promoted from being an usherette at the Invicta. This talkie age cinema started off with Western Electric high fidelity, replaced by Wide Range in April 1934. The Ernemann Mark Vs also gave way to non-water-cooled Mark IVs. The opening film was 'Monte Carlo' on the 12 October 1931. George Rase from the Strood Invicta joined William Croneen, son of Walter as joint manager.

The auditorium of the Plaza was classical in style with an ornate ceiling. It seated 1,804 originally, and on two occasions at least the famous joined the audience. Leslie Fuller and John Mills both came in whilst on location during 1936 and 1945 respectively. Quick off the mark with cinemascope, the Plaza had the pick of Fox 'scope pictures, exacting revenge on the circuit houses who had barred so much product in the past. The original Magnascope frame and screen tabs had to be hidden behind a false proscenium in order to handle 'The Robe'. Other features survived however, notably the polished wood entrance doors inset with bevelled glass, and the paybox with brass ticket plates and rose pattern security grille. A beautiful bronze brazier with genuine Louis XIV fire dogs at each corner, could be seen in the balcony lounge. The Plaza came to play mainly the ABC releases, but in 1966, Roy Squire of the Pavilion ballroom ran a part week bingo session until able to move to the Classic in 1977. Without bingo, the Plaza had 1,691 seats to fill, and sadly Michael Caine came for the last time 'Dressed To Kill' on the 29 November 1980. Workmen soon were converting the Plaza into dressing rooms, studios, offices and a restaurant for TV South. Upstairs, the walls were so thick they needed compressors! Jack Croneen, who had run the company since 1946, was invited together with four of his cinema staff, to the original opening on the 4 March 1982. By then, the original decor was masked by insulation cladding, but Mr Croneen said he was glad the place was still in use for entertainment.

Gillingham's last cinema was built by local fire chief and pawnbroker, Frederick White. He had met Bertie Garrett at the time of the Kings Hall fire, and decided that his expertise in exhibition would be useful for the rapidly built cinema in Gardiner Street. Mr Robert Cromie, later to design the Chatham Ritz, was responsible for the Gillingham **Embassy**, which included a first floor café/ballroom. An organ was not installed in the space provided. The cinema cost £40,000 and seated 1,750. Its design was of plain red brick and white stone, with a wide canopy and picture window above. The auditorium was finished in sprayed-on peach and gold with a futurist pattern on the ante-proscenium grilles. A stage and two dressing rooms completed the picture. Alderman H. A. Tye declared the Embassy open on the 4 October 1936, only 4 months since the laying of the foundation stone! Jane Caine, the girl with the golden voice, supplemented a double bill of 'Mr Deeds Goes To Town' and 'Don't Gamble With Love'.

Odeon Theatres took control on the 12 March 1938. They had a Saturday morning Mickey Mouse club for the children. Renamed the **Odeon** from the 16 June 1946, films came here after the 2 Medway town Gaumonts, but after the Chatham Gaumont closed, sometimes films ran in tandem with Rochester. Classic took over the lease in December 1967, but made no major changes, apart from wrestling and late night shows. As the Classic, a Tatler club was introduced in 1970 for such X-rated movies as 'Teenage Nympho'. Strippers could also appear, in the flesh. Leasehold status killed any talk of subdivision, and so Roy Squire, unable to have bingo fulltime at the Plaza, leased the Classic from Fred White's widow, and brought the club here from the 13 June 1977. He sold his Canterbury Street ballroom to Pleasurama who turned it into Joanna's discothe-

Chatham Ritz' magnificent 'café' (Premier Bioscope)

The Royal, Rainham, after closure in 1966 (CTA)

que. The cinema became the Embassy once more, and the Mary Lin School of Dancing moved into the old café area. The last film show had run on the 17 September 1977. A garish purple and yellow external colour scheme was later toned down to scarlet and cream, and the whole club upgraded by Coral, who took over early in 1986.

Church bells were said to be heard by audiences inside the Royal cinema, **RAINHAM**, just a few doors along the High Street from the parish church. Before the Royal, there was a more primitive hall on the site of the United Services Club. This iron and wood building charged 3d or 6d to admit patrons to see Charlie Chaplin, Pearl White or Eddie Cantor, on a screen flanked by potted palms. The doors were left open to light the interior before the children's Saturday matinees – to save on lighting perhaps? Heating too was minimal. The **Picture Palace**, or 'bug hutch' as it was better known, did not show black and white films, rather they were in 2 shades of grey, but the screen faded out altogether some time before the new Royal came on the scene.

The **Royal** was converted from a Salvation Army hall in 1923/24, and remained a very basic old-fashioned cinema for its first quarter of a century. Patrons entered from a passage on the right hand side, into a narrow foyer which led to an entrance near the screen, which faced the High Street. The small 395-seater was run by local men, who collected their films by van twice a week from London. (Many other Kent cinemas used the Castle Garage in Ramsgate). James Boyd put in new heating and projection in 1947, but 5 years later, the Royal was badly damaged by fire. Luckily it was bought by Mrs D. Glass of Darland, Gillingham, whose Darland Cinema Co. upgraded the cinema with new seating and a redecoration. Cinemascope followed in May 1956. Although a third run house where you could catch a film missed in the Medway towns, the latter-day Royal was superior in comfort to many rivals. However, a cash offer for the premises led to Miss Glass's retirement and the quiet closure of the cinema on the 5 March 1966, with 'Cat Ballou'. Vye and Son opened a small supermarket which later extended to adjacent premises. The whole area is now Gerald Lukehurst's furniture showroom.

SEVENOAKS

The first operators of cinemas in **SEVENOAKS** seem to have been at a loss when it came to coining distinctive names. They also had a predeliction to build on the same site – both a little confusing for the cinema historian. Travelling showmen began to screen pictures in the Club Hall, Dartford Road which accommodated 750. This hall was destroyed by an explosive bomb in 1940, but its cinematic life was curtailed by the news of full time establishments in prospect.

The **Palace**, Tubs Hill (or Electric Theatre), opened in Station Parade on the 6 January 1911, having had to wait over Christmas for a mislaid electrical part. There was a raked floor, velvet plush chairs and some musical accompaniment, but the hall was stuffy and cramped. Messrs Young & Son were soon proving the effectiveness of their automatic carpet cleaner on the Palace's well trodden carpets. Small boys took turns to crank the projector, reversing the handle for sheer devilment – until the untimely laughter from the audience alerted the irate manager. Meanwhile, a bank-like building called the Cinema Electric Theatre had been erected at 152 High Street by Mr Robinson, proprietor of the Royal Oak Hotel. Three panels on the façade promised comedy, travel and tragedy on the site of Smith's brewery. The auditorium was a long and narrow one without a gallery, and it seated 240 twice nightly plus Wednesday and Saturday afternoons. A 3d piece gained admittance, but wounded soldiers and Belgian army evacuees were soon to be admitted free to view 'interesting war topics' filmed by Gaumont Graphic.

Within a short time both these cinemas were rebuilt and enlarged. First in line was the High Street Cinema, which closed in May 1925. As architect Percy Potter worked on his Tudoresque replacement, patrons went back to the Club Hall, and then to premises behind it. Lord Sackville came to declare The Cinema opened again on the 26 of January, the public being admitted to see 'Peter Pan' on the morrow.

It was possible to seat 550, who were warmer and better ventilated, and had the choice of a balcony or boxes for four. Just in case of the dreaded conflagration, water sprinklers were on hand. Down at the Tubs Hill Palace, children ceased to hurl peanut shells at the pianist as their habitat came up for renewal. Here Charles Crabbe created a clean, uncluttered brick edifice praised by the author of 'Modern Theatres And Cinemas' for its workmanlike unpretentiousness. This was the second hall opened by the newly-formed Sevenoaks Cinema Co. and was a vast improvement on the old Palace. A better entrance, tip-ups and a new projection box at the rear of the hall raised the tone, but the auditorium was cosily limited to 400 seats. 'Michael Strogoff' played the Palace from the 7 November 1927.

Nearly to the Bat and Ball station, on the left side of St Johns Hill, there stood a plain hall with a high-pitched roof and central door, known as the New Theatre. By 1928, it was the **New Picture Theatre**, liberally decked with film billboards and banners. By now Sevenoaks had these 3 cinemas on the threshold of the sound era. The Tubs Hill Palace led on the 30 December 1929, booking 'Broadway Melody'. Advertisements now described this cinema as 'talking' and the one in the High Street as 'silent'. The latter waited until the 15 September 1930 to show 'Condemned' on Western Electric apparatus. This system soon replaced the more basic Syntock installed at Tubs Hill. Last in line, St Johns Hill spoke (or sung?) on the 3 November when Maurice Chevalier starred in 'The Innocents of Paris'.

When a national chain showed interest in the Royal Crown Hotel site, Sevenoaks Cinemas decided on a pre-emptive strike, although the initial plans for London Road were rejected. The High Street cinema was replaced yet again after closing the Tudoresque building in May 1935. St Johns Hill reacted too, for they closed for remodelling on the 24 June. Back in business first, Councillor R. Robinson, chairman of both the UDC and rival Sevenoaks Cinemas, came to declare the **Carlton** open on the 23 September. Now the area had a proper cinema, with canopy, a modern appearance and 350 seats – 70 of these in the balcony. The prestigious architect, the late David Evelyn Nye was engaged for the High Sreet reconstruction. The name 'The Cinema' carved on the frontage was hardly new, but novelties abounded – a cafe with teak floor, and a 5-rank 2-manual Compton on a lift with ornamental surround. There were fibrous plaster lighting troughs, a neon sign outside and a box running Kalees and Western Electric. Lord Sackville returned on the 4 November 1935, when a full house saw Mickey Mouse, 'The Private Lives Of The Gannets', Gracie Fields in 'Look Up And Laugh' and Herbert Small at the organ.

Despite an apparent extra capacity in the town, the council licensed Cohen and Raper to build in London Road. There was room for George Coles to provide an impressive frontage for the **Majestic**, dominated by large but purely decorative arched windows. As at the Cinema, there was a restaurant and car park. The foyer had a vitreous enamel floor and paybox flush with the wall. The cinema held 1,250 (750 + 500), the circle having its own lounge. Green, gold, scarlet and bronze flecking brightening the auditorium whose seats were in 'vieux rose'. The box had a 135-ft throw to the screen on which Rear Admiral Elliot and the first night audience saw 'When Nights Were Bold' on the 22 August 1936. Attending their needs the patrons had usherettes in grey trousers with blue piping and lido blue blouses. These had a large gold bow at the back.

This competition forced the Tubs Hill cinema to close on the 19 December 1936, but it became a repertory theatre, using the 13-ft deep stage and 3 dressing rooms to the full now. Rep died on these boards, so Herbert's Motorcycle Store and then a heating engineers occupied the premises. Now a sub-branch of Barclays stands facing the railway station. Sevenoaks Cinemas sold their High Street cinema to Lou Morris, who christened it **Plaza**. Herbert Small became organist/manager, but only 2 months later, Cohen and Raper took over the lease and subsequently the freehold at an auction held in June 1937. Despite all this provision, Union were thinking of coming to Sevenoaks, but their declining fortunes brought the same non-event as in Strood.

Further takeovers ensued – Odeon took over the Majestic in 1943, and Granada the Plaza during 1947. Respectively renamed after the circuits, Sevenoaks had an **Odeon** from July 1945 and a **Granada** in November 1947. As the fifties dawned, the Carlton rang the changes to stay afloat. It became the New Carlton Theatre in September 1950, with live shows and a pantomime, then a cinema again next February. As such it closed and re-opened, this time under Anthony O'Brien. He called it the Embassy. Continental, art and revival films were run, but interest flagged and aging heating and projection could not be overhauled. The last house came on the 14 February 1954. Bolter's surgical and dental supplies moved in, but the canopy and iron staircase to the box are still preserved. Next to go was the Granada, which went dark in October 1960 with Sylvia Sims in 'No Trees In The Street' but the street, in the form of a new road, prevailed and the Granada has gone.

If you follow this tale, only the Odeon is left unclosed. Despite its solo situation, tripling was deemed necessary and its 1,442 seats became 450 + 104 + 106 in a standard Rank tripling (1972). Brent Walker leased the cinema from them in October 1975 – note the BW monogram on the door handles. As the Focus, the lease expired on the last day of October 1982, but in the nick of time, **ACE** (Alternative Cinema Entertainments) took over on that day. Although the ACE twins hold the cinema fort in the divided stalls, the main auditorium is now the Stag Theatre, after Sevenoaks Theatre Action Group. STAG obtained ready-made premises in a deal signed in 1983. The District Council paid over £250,000 to Rank to secure a 50-year lease of building and car park until 2034. Two art forms now replace one, not forgetting a video games centre filling some space behind screen 2.

The Tudoresque cinema on busy Hosey Hill, **WESTERHAM**, is no more. It originated as a venture promoted by the local brewery, then run by Messrs Bushell, Watkins and Smith. The cinema was open before the Great War, and known not inappropriately, as the **Swan**. In the inter-war years, it was managed for much of this period by Captain Outwin. A 16mm operation, the small box was equipped in latter years with Kalee 7 projection and BT-H sound. The Swan seated only 300, with two small balconies on either side of the protruding box. The two balconies fell into disuse, no doubt because of stricter fire regulations. Cut to 160 seats, the cinema continued from 1956 as the **Tudor**, recalling its applied half-timbered frontage. The motto of the town cinema was 'Nothing is too much trouble for the Tudor'. Patronage fell and the Tudor closed at the end of 1963. There were plans to re-open in the spring, but arson on the 2 April, 1964 ruined the project. The box, cash desk and offices were destroyed. The whole building came down in 1970.

The oddly named **Negresco Cinema** still stands in **EDENBRIDGE** High Street as premises for Cheverton Antiques. I understand the cinema may have been a public hall, but was adapted and refronted as the Cinema, opening as such on the 30 December 1927. Its proprietors were then the Adelphi Advertising Co., but by 1938 a Mr Milner was running the 330-seat cinema, and calling it the

Sevenoaks Granada, under its original name, c.1935 (CTA)

The Tudor, Westerham, in the early 1960s

Negresco. Perhaps he was inspired by the famous French hotel of that name? There was a café, which predeceased the cinema, whose last advert was for 'Rockets Galore' in February 1959. The proscenium width was only 16 feet, so maybe the building served better as a supermarket before the present antiques business expanded into its confines.

SWANLEY now the first town across the boundary from the London Borough of Bromley, had developed enough before the war to deserve its own cinema. Built in London Road near Swanley Junction on the site of Swanley Hall, the cinema has been variously named the Swanley cinema or the **Corona**. At the time of closure the advert for the last film was headed 'Swanley' but the press preferred to describe it as the Corona. At the time of opening on the 6 October 1938 it was hailed by the mayor of Dartford as the first cinema in their rural district. The cinema was designed by Sykes and Pomfret of Eltham for the joint proprietors F. Rainbow and D. C. Pruden. Seating was for about 900 with provision of stage and equipment for occasional variety turns. The opening film, 'A Yank At Oxford' was shown and the 2-manual Compton Theatrone christened by Reginald New. Eldred Skinner, one of New's pupils and a local church organist, was also present to accompany songs from the tenor David Knight. He stayed for some years as resident organist.

The Corona was later managed by G. Downs, who also acquired the Rex at Borough Green. Cinemascope was installed, the proscenium width being adequate to take the new 31-foot wide screen. Although the population of the town gradually increased, takings fell and in the last decade or so as a cinema, only 350 seats were in use. Under the management of Charles Crathorne, two nights of bingo were introduced. However, a change of policy was announced, by which the cinema became a full-time club except for Saturday children's matinees. The last adult film show was a double bill of 'Scorching Sands' and 'Hell Below Deck' on Saturday, 22 November 1965, after which two children's matinees were advertised – then silence. Plans were finally appoved for a new Civic Centre which opened its doors in April 1973.

Folkestone Playhouse in the early 1950s (CTA)

SHEPWAY

As a major resort, **FOLKESTONE** had plenty of existing entertainment buildings available for the bioscope. Space precludes a detailed history here. The Town Hall (1861) exhibited films from the Anglo-French and American Syndicate. The Victoria Pier Pavilion (1887–1954) tried everything to entice 1,000 people to cross the shore line, including, from 1908, motion pictures. The later Marine Gardens Pavilion and the subterranean Leas Hall have also shown documentaries which did not compete with the commercial cinema. The former **Pleasure Gardens** in Bouverie Road (1888–1964) remained a live entertainment venue, even when run by Walter Bentley of the Central and Playhouse Cinemas, and subsequently by Union Cinemas. However, from November 1956, this theatre began its last days as a fulltime cinema. Despite new projection equipment and seating, and the removal of some obstructive pillars, not enough people were attracted out of the town centre for its mainly continental programming. Organ enthusiasts should note that a 2-rank 5-unit Compton had been acquired from the Rex, Cambridge in 1949. After the last film show in May 1964, the Pleasure Gardens Theatre was demolished.

In Grace Hill, Players Motor Garage (1902, subsequently a skating rink) was adapted into a 400-seat one-floor cinema. Patrons were admitted from the 3rd of May 1910 and were soon witnessing, on celluloid, the funeral of King Edward VII. Renamed **Savoy** in 1927, the old garage announced in the following September, 1928 that talking films were coming to Kent. However, this only meant audible shorts depicting song and dance routines – the main features were still quiet. Shortly after one of these – 'Fire' a real one gutted the cinema on the 13 December! The owners, Mrs O'Connor and her son, were luckily able to use the insurance to rebuild a more refined Super New Savoy with no less than 954 seats. The Savoyards enjoyed a first floor café with an aerated soda fountaina and palm lounge, and the cinema had added a 2-manual 7-rank Dutch Standaart organ. Re-opening after the 28 week pause took place on 29 June 1929. The attractions were 'The Burgomaster of Stilemonde', John Russell and his Orchestra and Percy Milton on the Dutch organ – Percy was a demonstrator for Standaart.

Full length talkies began in earnest on the 2nd of September with 'Broadway Melody'. The O'Connors upgraded the sound system with Western Electric in 1931. When Dover Entertainments (who ran the Kings Hall there) took over, they concentrated on enhancing the organ. To do this, the console was repositioned centrally, given a new glass surround and pedal board, and celebrities like Reginald Foort booked for guest appearances. The Savoy survived the war, although closed for 10 months by heavy air raids until the 13 May 1941. However, one unfortunate schoolboy was killed when a ventilation motor fell from the ceiling on top of him. His distraught mother was with him: years later her ghost alarmed the staff! Part week bingo was introduced in October 1961 and took over completely after the 'Gargon Terror' scared away all the remaining cinema patrons on the 18 April 1962. Star bingo and Rio bingo played on until 1984, but latterly all is silent. As for the Standaart, local C.O.S. member E. R. Hart painstakingly removed the instrument to his home, saving the Savoy sound for true believers.

The shortlived **Queens** Cinema, 78 Tontine Street, had less staying power. Opened in June 1912 with 400 seats, a raked floor and motorised projection, it was handicapped by pillars cutting sight lines. Prices too were cut, but to no avail. Closed by 1917, the Queens became a Temperance Hall, then by 1937, Day by Day Printers. After the war, a plastics factory took over, and the building still survives in 2 gabled sections separated by a flat mid-section with central entrance.

Encouraged by the Electric's success, its owners bought up Ivy House and adjacent stables to make way for the **Playhouse**. This fine cinema, faced in Bath stone, was the design of A. R. Bowles. One of his characteristic glass-topped verandahs supported on 4 cast-iron pillars shaded the entrance. This had the name 'Playhouse' in stained glass, floodlit by night or embellished by hanging baskets of flowers by day. It being only the 14th of August 1912, the thick pile carpets and tip-up seating much impressed the press. Continuous performances included the Gaumont Graphic and variety turns on stage. A band was engaged to play in the tea room from 1928. This was entirely furnished by Bobby's department store. In 1929, Walter Bentley, a London variety agent, acquired both Playhouse and Central, and ordered the former an organ to compete with the Savoy. Here an all British Compton was the choice (2-manual 5-ranks). This had the curious provision of a tremulant on the outside wall which annoyed neighbours so much that a silencing box was fitted. Harold Meredith's console was hopefully, more conventionally sited! To stay up-to-date, a Panotrope was installed in 1929, to accompany 'Lucky Boy' 5 months later in December, the Savoy went all the way with Western Electric and the talkie 'Speakeasy' (how apt!). Now, the organ, hidden in the orchestra pit with a single cramped chamber, languished in obscurity.

Bentley died, and both Playhouse and Central found their way via Union Cinemas to ABC. Closed for the duration until the 1 April 1946, the Playhouse resumed minus the café. Mirrophonic sound was introduced, but during its postwar existence under Essoldo, business ebbed away until the last reel – 'I Thank A Fool' went through the gate on the 25 August 1962. Sadly the building and most of the organ were dismantled the following May, and an undistinguished supermarket put in its place.

Folkestone's last cinema was also among the first, flickering into life in George Lane on the 23 September 1912. Today's very different Cannon triple was then the **Central Picture Theatre**, seating somewhat under 900 in fauteuils, stalls and benches. In the latter half of 1921, both box and roof ascended a further floor, giving the cinema an extra tier and a capacity of 1,500. A resident orchestra under the direction of Phil Bekker entertained in the closing silent years, but 'Bulldog Drummond' could speak for himself in October 1929. By then, the Central had joined forces with the rival Playhouse under a new company – Amalgamated

Folkestone Cinemas Ltd. Walter Bentley kept both AFC cinemas in the public eye by extensive advertising and attractive programming. Talkies were the excuse to extensively refurbish the Central, bringing capacity down to 1,351. After Bentley died in 1935, his company sold out to Union in 1936, who in turn merged with ABC.

In wartime, visitors were excluded, but the armed forces and locals justified a star-studded premier of the H. G. Wells classic, 'Kipps' in May 1941. When Essoldo took over in April 1946, they waited 10 years before changing the name. Classic acquired Essoldo cinemas in March 1972, and the cinema immediately became the Classic. Between November 1973 and March 1974, the cinema was closed entirely whilst work went on creating 3 auditoria in the space occupied by the old triple deck Essoldo. The triplets, ascending from 1 to 3, held 291, 308 and 196 respectively, the last and uppermost opening on the 23 May. Shortly afterwards, Classic's former chairman Eric Rhodes, took over the Folkestone complex, renaming it Curzon for the ensuing 10 years. In 1984, Classic were back, promising that their greater booking strength would bring new releases here sooner. Restructured as the Cannon group, the Folkestone **Cannon** belongs to the UK's largest cinema circuit.

Folkestone's only really super cinema was the **Astoria**, Sandgate Road. Major C. H. Bell, managing director of Astoria (Folkestone) Ltd., engaged E. F. Stone to design the 1,670 seat Astoria. Replacing the Central Restaurant, the new super was in a down-town shopping area although not over prominent architecturally. However, ample vestibule and cloakroom accommodation had been provided, also a downstairs waiting area, useful in wet weather. There was a restaurant directly accessible from the street, open all day, with ancillary cocktail bar and a small dance floor. Naturally, a big organ was called for – a 3-manual 6-rank Compton. The Astoria was dual purpose, its mahogany laid stage being 20-ft deep and fully equipped for stage shows. Vertical decorative grills flanked the proscenium, these were lit by rows of tungsten lights. Concealed lighting prevailed elsewhere. Higher up than even the 2nd floor kichen, the box was equipped with Western Electric and BT-H apparatus.

Being Easter Saturday, on the 20 April 1935, a page boy was delegated to being an easter egg on stage to inaugurate the Astoria. Would a film called 'The Gay Divorce' open a cinema now? Or one about the private life of the gannet, which also played the Sevenoaks Majestic? 'We cannot afford to give away entertainment' said Major Bell, so admission was never below 9d after 3 p.m. Little stage entertainment was offered after the first year – examples of who did come were Younkman and his Czardas Band and the Tom Katz Saxophone Six. The organ was well used, with many guest appearances. Stage manager, Peter Colley created sets purely for organ solos.

Associated Theatres acquired the Astoria in 1936. As an associate of County Cinemas, they improved film quality. County managed the Astoria from October 1936 until merged with Odeon in 1937. The name **Odeon** was used from June 1940. Before this, however, in 1938, the Astoria had been the venue for the annual conference of the Cinema Exhibitors' Association. CEA members saw new films after regular patrons had left, but ironically most came on release to competing cinemas! As at the Savoy, there was a wartime casualty when a soldier was hit by a stray bullet coming from a dog fight somewhere overhead. 'Monty' addressed his troops here as they prepared for D-Day. Thereafter, the economics of super cinemas gradually worsened. Rank renovated the auditorium, tried out amateur dramatics on stage and turned the restaurant into the Sandgate Bar and Disco. The last great occasion was a charity performance of 'West Side Story' in aid of the Order of St John in Kent. A packed house also heard Gerald Shaw at the organ, Harry Leader and his Orchestra and some comedy from Norman Wisdom. The end came on the 26 January 1974 with a double James Bond bill. Today, Boots stands on the site, and the organ was last heard of in Holland.

In suburban **CHERITON**, the **Electric Hall** stood at the junction of Chilham Road with High Street. Opened on the 8 August 1911, the proprietor claimed to put the world before your eyes – or tea upon your lap, threepenny seats excepted! A Mr A. O. Sherren designed the 400-seat Electric, which also featured variety under the alias, Palace Theatre. Both entertainments regaled the troops from nearby Shorncliffe Camp until May 1924. Thereafter, part of the premises served as Headleys (grocers) until 1950. Now a Jet petrol station marks the site. There was also a short-lived 16mm operation in the **St Martin's Hall**, High Street for a few years after the Second World War.

At 101–103 High Street, **SANDGATE**, a music hall earned itself several names, including, unofficially, The Bricks. In 1925, Councillor Maltby was claiming that it had seen the first cinematograph exhibition outside London – in 1894. Be that as it may, Edwards Imperial Bioscope played there before the Great War. During the latter, the then Alhambra served as a YMCA for Canadian forces. In 1921, the Bricks became the **Sandgate Picture House**. At the date in question, there were 2 shops flanking the portico entrance and a large flat at first floor level. Architect A. R. Bowles provided a wood panelled foyer with paybox and manager's office leading to a 514-seat auditorium (374 + 140). The proscenium opening, with ornamental plaster surround, measured 17 ft 6 in wide, with an orchestra pit at the base.

South Coast Cinemas ran the Picture House, which opened on the 1 June, but closed before the end of 1921 due to insolvency. A buyer eventually was found, and the cinema resumed on the 20 September 1925. It was then that councillor Maltby made his claim for Sandgate already mentioned. Films were shown nightly plus Wednesday and Saturday afternoons. A Sunday licence was sought, but a non-religious objection was received, namely that the generator was ruining wireless reception! This was resolved and the licence granted. Sandgate's big moment came in April 1929 when 'King Of Kings' was banned in Folkestone but played here. Sound however did not reach Sandgate until June 1930. In 1939, the newly renamed **Rex** closed for the duration, as it backed on to a possible invasion beach. The threat long over, business resumed on the 2 June

1949, but only until the 9 June 1951, when 'Joan Of Arc' met her fate. The Rex was put to commercial use and then became Rayner's Beach Club in the sixties.

HYTHE has gained and lost 4 cinemas. The first at 111 High Street was on the site of the burned down Sportsman public house. The **Picture Palace** opened on the 12 April 1911, still minus heating, but boasting a dome-shaped paybox covered in gold leaf and a set of marble steps to the 450-seat interior. Khaki-clad Canadians boosted admissions in the Great War, which were even allowed on Sundays. Still silent, the Picture Palace closed on the 9 April 1927, its staff transferring to its successor, the Grove. A shopping arcade on the site was itself bombed in the last war, so modern shops mark the site almost opposite Theatre Street.

The **Grove**, Prospect Road was aptly named as it stood behind two oaks, up a path of evergreens. The architect, A. E. Palmer designed a one-floor hall on the corner of Mount Street. It held 650, and had pinewood block flooring and an orange and light blue colour scheme. The mayor attended the opening on 16 May 1927, and thenceforth part-week bookings supplemented by Harold Taylor and his Orchestra took the Grove up to talkies. These came with 'Flight' in May 1930. Western Electric Mirrorphonic sound was brought in during July 1937. Soon, more troops were in town, and the Grove carried on despite suffering roof damage. By now, London & Provincial Cinemas had taken over from Hythe Picture Palace (1913) Ltd. It was L. & P.C. who decided in leaner times to fall back on their later Ritz, and to close down the Grove on the 1 March 1958. Three of the staff from the original cinema were still at the Grove when it closed with James Cagney in 'Man Of A Thousand Faces'. The Grove subsequently became a car showroom.

Next in line was a circuit house for Union Cinemas. The **Ritz** was built at the junction of Prospect Road and East Street. The plainish exterior has a bow-shaped canopy leading into a vestibule. In turn this leads up a few steps to a foyer with paybox. Financial stringencies caused space for a café to be unused, and the opening ceremony itself on the 12 June 1937 was uncharacteristically low key. With 858 seats, the Ritz was Hythe's largest cinema, but still compact. Ornamental insets, back-lit and draped with heavy satin, were a feature of the auditorium. 'Keep Your Seats Please' starring George Formby was Union's first film for the Ritz, but as elsewhere, it was soon ABC in control. They disposed of the Ritz to London & Provincial Cinemas in March 1953 – L. & P.C. already had the Grove. In 1966, the Ritz was under Mecca management and became solely a bingo club from 1966 until July 1971. Films were then reinstated in a circle only cinema holding 276, whilst Vogue bingo played on below. From 1982, Classic acquired the lease, but were unable to find enough suitable films for the local audience. By 1984, returns were not even covering staff wages some weeks. The author was in one of the last queues – to see 'E.T.' – but by then queues were a rarity. On the 7 August 1984 the Classic, as it was then, locked up with 'Indiana Jones And The Temple Of Doom'.

The least known of Hythe's cinemas was a 16mm operation known as the

Embassy. Sited in a modern one-floor building next to the R.H.&D.R. station, this 100-seater only operated between 1970 and 1972.

Details of the Romney Marsh area are a little sketchy. The consensus is that **DYMCHURCH** had at least one cinema, the **Dymchurch Picture House**, which one source says opened in August 1914. The photograph suggests a turn of the century public hall adapted for pictures. Although quite small, the building dwarfed the row of shops and Midland Bank, all constructed of wood and corrugated iron, besides which it stood. The East Kent Road Car Co. had a bus rank nearby. Films played here until about 1932, after which the building became an ice cream parlour with a few tables set out for teas. A later photograph of the hall shows it as the 'Sports Arena' (admission free), where slot machines could be played. On the 24 August 1940, the old cinema and its neighbours were wrecked by a German bomb and not rebuilt. Another building in Eastbridge Street may have been used as a cinema, possibly the single-storey Marshlands Hotel, also bombed in 1940.

A dance hall in **NEW ROMNEY** began life as the Pavilion Picture Palace. Sited between Buckhurst House and the Ship Inn, the proprietor of the latter, Harry Merritt introduced films in about 1923. The Pavilion seated a mere 100, and its tiny 5 by 10-ft box housed Power and Pathe machines. Later, it was run by D. Paine, son of Thomas Paine, the Lydd cinema entrepreneur. Nearby at **LITTLESTONE-ON-SEA**, the Army Kinematograph Corporation put on film shows at the Perks Hall in the last war. Sir Robert Perks was responsible for bringing the railway to New Romney in 1884.

In **LYDD**, an old tithe barn on the Rype was converted into a cinema in 1912. Known locally as The Barn, or officially as **Ye Olde Picturedrome**, the enterprising conversion was executed by farmer, Thomas William Paine. Around 1921, films were displaced by skating – the reverse of the trend elsewhere. Sadly, this historic property was struck by lightning in 1936 and later pulled down. Paine and Balcombe, another farmer, joined forces with a local photographer to build a cinema in Lydd. Its opening in about 1916, was no doubt the cause of the barn's re-use. Built by Ellis Bros. of New Romney, the cinema was modest in size with 303 seats, and more centrally sited in the High Street. A New Romney man, William Eugene McCormack took it over in 1922, christening the cinema the Playhouse. McCormack had a longish journey to Lydd station with the nightly takings, which he took to his home at Littlestone-on-Sea. The Playhouse's main claim to fame is when it premiered a locally shot movie called 'The Loves Of Joanne Godden'. Equipped with AWH sound, the Lydd cinema lived on, sustained by the local army garrison. However, Mr McCormack sold out to a film distribution company in 1959. In the final years the name **Regal** or Cinema seem to have been interchangeable, but in February 1963 the cinema was up for sale. Closed by 1964, the site is now occupied by fire brigade premises.

Lydd Picturedrome (right), c.1923 (Doris Goodsell)

The Dymchurch Picture House in the 1930s (Doris Goodsell)

Hythe Embassy, c.1970 (CTA)

A rare view of the New Romney Cinema

Three out of four **FAVERSHAM** cinemas can still be found in the town. The first to open, in quiet Tanners Street, was a converted school. Walter Charles Wilson, who also ran the Star, Tonbridge, had the Faversham **Empire** under way during 1910. His first films included 'A Story Of Tomatoes' and 'Dog Waiter'. This animal, vegetable but not mineral fare could be sampled for 2d, 3d or 4d. The Empire stayed in business until 1935, when it was superseded by East Kent Cinemas' new Argosy super. The Empire is now a catholic church.

Knightsbridge furnishers occupy the old **Gem** cinema in Preston Street, but the scrollery and escallop feature at first-floor level hint at the building's past. No. 19A opened as a cinema in 1912, and survived into the talkie era by acquiring Kalee 8s and BT-H sound in 1930. Even closer to the Argosy, it was also eclipsed and closed in 1935. Subsequently converted into a store, it was the home of Alexander Sloan and still offers 3,500 square feet of sales space for selling furniture.

The heiress to the 2 halls above was the **Argosy**, which stood up a passage almost opposite the Gem. Leslie Carter and F. E. Bromige designed the new super for East Kent Cinemas. Only semi-visible from Preston Street, the exterior was unremarkable, relying on a brightly-lit and well advertised approach to attract patrons. The Argosy seated 788 (658 + 130). Lighting in the vestibule was provided by 6 V-shaped ceiling fittings, plus 2 wall brackets, and the auditorium had 14 wall brackets, all sprayed in harmony with the decor. The Argosy opened on the 4 February 1935 with a Gracie Fields classic – 'Sing As We Go' reproduced on BT-H apparatus. Renamed **Regal** in 1950, the cinema was subsequently acquired by the Peter Lindsay Group, who dropped films entirely in favour of bingo during 1965. When Joe Coral Holdings acquired both Regal and Royal from Lindsay in November 1973, the latter was also running bingo 2 nights per week. Coral rationalised, closing the Regal entirely in March 1974. Planning permission for a Lipton supermarket was granted in February 1978 and demolition soon took place. The present supermarket has advanced forward to the street line.

Last in date, but not in looks, the **Odeon** 9 Market Street, alias Middle Row, has a medieval appearance. Leaded windows and a dainty steeple surmounted by a Garten and Thorne weather vane are not the usual Odeon accessories. The Camden Town firm also installed the vomitory rails and showcases, according to a detailed list in the opening programme. Andrew Mather extended the Tudoresque treatment into the half-timbered stadium style auditorium. Ignoring the period however, the opening publicity boasted that 'every known means of art, science and hygiene have been introduced to further the comfort of patrons'. The 'wonderful new system of coloured lighting' came into play on the 'exquisitely tinted curtain' on the 9 March 1936. The 729-seat cinema remained an Odeon until leased to Classic with many others in December 1967. The change was shortlived, for Peter Lindsay was here with part-week bingo

◊
The Royal, Faversham, before films ceased in 1985

◊
The 1912-vintage Queen's Theatre, Sittingbourne

from 1969. As the Royal (or Royle if we believe the yellow pages!) film attendances fell to 20–30 per night. After the lease passed to Coral in November 1973, they opted for bingo in one building. This took effect from the 1 May 1974. Five thousand, seven hundred petititioners opposed the loss of films, but were not queuing to get in at the time, alas.

The Royal was not greatly altered as a bingo hall, and still had some late night and children's matinees until 1977. Seating had now been cut back to 463. Herbert Kean, a new leaseholder and managing director of Herband Cinemas, reintroduced films for four nights a week in January 1979, but stated that late night shows had caused vandalism, so would not be run. This cine-bingo pattern lasted until the 8 June 1985, when films again ceased. Lack of support and the barring exercised by Canterbury and Sittingbourne were blamed. The New Royal bingo club is quietly situated only yards from the market place of this heritage-filled town, and does not disgrace it.

The Empire Picture Hall, **SITTINGBOURNE** has been demolished, but the former Wesleyan school became a cinema from the 20 July 1910. Its proprietors, Messrs Walter Charles Wilson and Wicks seem to be everywhere – the author encountered them in Chesham in an earlier book. The property at 72 East Street had its own generator run off a 5 h.p. gas engine. This worked hard, for soon the police were asking for some control to be exercised on the waiting queues! When they passed inside, a raked floor and tip-up seats were soon to reward their continued custom. Around 1930, East Kent Cinemas took over and renamed the cinema **Empire**. They probably made more concrete changes, for the plain stucco front with **Plaza** in relief looks of thirties origin. The capacity rose to 469 and a 10-ft deep stage and two dressing rooms were added. However, this out of centre cinema was an early casualty, closing with 'Honeychile' on the 9 August 1952. There was talk of using the Plaza as a sports hall, but after it was finally sold to the U.D.C. in November 1972, it was demolished and replaced by flats – Plaza Court. These can be found opposite the Assembly of God church.

Both the Empire and the Drill Hall (which was also used on occasions for film performances) objected to a cinematograph licence being granted to an old brewery just off the High Street. To no avail, for the **Queens Picture Theatre** opened on the 21 February 1912. Longevity later enabled it to claim, like many others, to be among the oldest still operating in Britain. Much earlier, the first manager, F. S. Brooks claimed it was the first to use a mirror type of arc lamp. In May 1912 a bijou orchestra was installed (violin, cello and piano). The Empire countered with the assertion: 'Our pictures are second to none on this earth'. At its height the Queens seated 653, who found their way in under an arch flanked by posters.

Little changed externally, Watchester Cinemas closed the Queens for a month during which screen, stage and sound were renewed. Redecoration, recarpeting and proscenium arch widening also took place – all in 1968. Business resumed on Sunday, 2 February, with approval granted to start on Sundays from 1.30 p.m. Morning shows for shift workers were also billed, admission only 1/–.

However, Classic were now operating in the former Odeon, and so films were dropped in 1973. £62,000 was spent to provide a live 392-seat theatre with new foyer, seats, lighting and dressing rooms. However, as few as 15 people came to performances and the theatre folded on the 10 April 1976. Expecting Mecca to devote the Odeon entirely to bingo, businessman Ray Sutton invested £10,000 re-equipping the Queens as a cinema. He had got as far as advertising 'Picnic At Hanging Rock' as the opener on the 4 March 1978, when Classic invoked a covenant forbidding film shows in the Queens. Instead, the Queens became Cleo's night club from the 14 February 1980. Sold by Bill Holman within 3 months, the club tried again under Jarvis Enterprises as Marteen's Night Spot. The ill-fated Queens had a serious fire in September 1981, but re-opened as a discotheque the following May.

The **Odeon** in the High Street has a complex history. Built on a corner site near the Parish church, its main entrance is on a mid curve of the frontage. The Odeon was designed for the circuit by F. C. Mitchell and held 1,593 (1,077 + 516) which was huge for Sittingbourne, but cost just £28,720. Lord and Lady Harris and the band of the Royal Engineers were there for the opening on the 4 January 1937. The band from Chatham played an overture to the film 'Little Lord Fauntleroy'. Curiously, it was another version of this film which was shown in April 1981, as a nostalgic gesture to the patrons who were at the 1937 ceremony. Unusually for Odeon, an organ was mooted, but the pit dug for the console struck the local bourne – hence no organ! The interior was restrained art deco, and a café was included which survived until the mid-fifties. This Odeon was disposed of to Classic in December 1967, but the cinema, now named Vogue, closed on the 13 January 1968. As Vogue bingo played in the stalls area, the Queens enjoyed 3½ years as sole picture house.

In August 1971, the fanfare of the Romford Drum and Trumpet Corps heralded Classic's first auditorium – a 111–seat mini fashioned from the old café. A larger 330-seater occupying the old circle followed during 1972 as promised. This had cost £40,000 as the foundations of the cinema needed strengthening. Vogue bingo was still in vogue downstairs. When Mecca acquired the whole building, they planned to run it exclusively as a social club. Consent was refused, and so cinema remains here instead of at the Queens. A dual operation – Mecca bingo and Cannon cinemas above can be visited using the respective halves of the partitioned corner entrance.

1985 was probably the swansong of cinema in Sheppey. Of the centres which have known film palaces, **SHEERNESS** is still of much interest. Oldest surviving building is an ex-servicemen's club and vacated 'Batharama' below in the Towers Hall, 150 High Street. This became the **Electric Theatre** on the 29 June 1911. Open in time to witness George V's coronation procession, the Electric could draw the curious to a film made in Leysdown by Pathe Freres. 'Fate Of A King' used 100 actors and was a phenomenal length. When acquired by the owners of the Oxford Picture Hall, the Electric closed for redecoration, new seating and heating. It was to re-open as the **Cambridge** cinema, but apparently never did so. The **Arcadia Cinema**, also in the High Street, was a narrow one-floor hall, seating about 200. This was open by 1913. This too had its special attractions, one such booked at normal prices during May 1915 was 'Tillie's Punctured Romance'. However, on this great occasion, the rear 3 rows could be reserved for 1/–. The Arcadia was run by Messrs Johnson and Rudd, but after James Chapman took over in 1921, he renamed the cinema the Casino. Chapman had good experience having managed the New Gallery, Regent Street. His successor, Charles Dyke planned further modernisation with a re-opening on the 2 July 1923, but as at the Cambridge, the day never came. The now demolished **Hippodrome Theatre**, Broadway, or erstwhile **Victoria Hall/Victoria Palace** commenced life in 1872. It was remodelled and reopened on Boxing Day 1920 as a cine-variety hall. When films were shown, the footlights were lowered, to afford an 'uninterrupted view of the sheet'. The entrance was Jacobean, with suitably leaded lights in the paybox. The auditorium had semi-indirect lighting, and plenty of velvet – for seats, door drapes and stage curtains. A £2,000 pipe organ was also present. Films became more important with talkies. A team working round the clock enlarged the operating, battery and generator rooms ready for Western Electric sound. The Hippodrome was not alone in beginning with 'The Singing Fool' – in November 1929. In later years, all the surviving cinemas passed to Lou Morris, and subsequently to Essoldo. They singled out this older hall for closure first, and demolition followed in 1970.

Several arcade shops and an upper floor café and carpet showroom occupy the **Oxford** cinema. Designed by F. H. Dore of Canterbury for the locally based Oxford Electric Theatre Co., this cinema was an advance on the two in the High Street. A canopy for wet weather, foyer, electric ventilation, steam gas radiators and dual gas and electric lighting justify my assertion. The box was reasonably large for one operator, and the rake steep enough to permit ladies to retain their hats. A restful white, French grey and gold decor was the company's choice – the choice of colour schemes in cinemas seem to be of infinite variety! A private show for wounded ex-servicemen took place on the 11 December 1916, after which the silent screen reigned supreme until 1929. Then, some missing synchronisers delayed the RCA sound installation for a whole week. Volunteers drove frantically all night to Leeds to draw fresh parts for despatch by rail in time for the big night on the 28 October. However, the new supers slowly killed business and the Oxford closed on the 25 July 1937. In the sixties, we find the premises in Russell Street trading as the Oxford Bingo Hall, seating 300 instead of 600. However, a fire in April 1977 badly damaged the ground floor and part of the roof. Next, the entrance was fitted with roller shutters to protect the Sheppey Microcomputer Centre. However, the present Oxford Shopping Arcade permits easier access, and the surviving curve of the ceiling in the furnishings area can be readily perceived as an early picture house, by the visitor.

1936–37 saw a massive increase in cinema seating in Sheerness. On Broadway at the Strode Crescent Junction, the **Argosy** opened up on the 29 January 1936.

Rather squat in my opinion, the main feature of F. E. Bromige's design is the hexagonal corner tower, which is less striking, viewed from the town centre. East Kent Cinemas gave the town 1,250 seats in which to see the first film, 'Brewster's Millions'. It was the first real super, and lasted until 1968, when the then owners, Essoldo, were pruning their circuit countrywide. The Argosy had a stage 12-ft deep, and displayed somewhat less prominently the thirties curved glass favoured by Bromige at his other cinemas, notably the Ace, Rayners Lane. After a longer spell as a Ladbroke Lucky 7 bingo club, the Argosy now trades as Fairways in the same cause.

The **Rio**, Broadway is undoubtedly the most spectacular. Its massive George Coles front would dominate any main street. It was natural that East Kent Cinemas and Cinema House Ltd (Hippodrome), claimed that Sheerness, with 23,000 souls had enough cinemas already, but Kay Bros. got their 1,600 seat addition approved and built. The original name was to be Royal, after the adjacent hotel, part of which had to be demolished. However, the name 'Rio' appeared on the vertical fin in the middle of the floodlit curve above the canopy. Patrons admired the 60-ft façade and passed through 5 sets of double doors into the spacious foyer. A circular tea room could be visited beneath the circular tower capping the front elevation. All this space and luxury proved first an inducement then a liability, so when Essoldo inherited the dinosaur from Lou Morris, it was here that they began their cut-backs. Closed quietly by 1958, the interior dwarfed some Lilliput Toys (children's typewriters etc.) until September 1980, but a 'for sale' board was the subsequent long running attraction outside this over-confident cinema.

Another super completed the cycle. On 15 March 1937, the more modest **Ritz** presented its faience fronted welcome to its first patrons. This Lou Morris theatre was designed by Edmund Walford of Leicester, who used ¾ million bricks to complete his 1,300-seater in only 20 weeks. The long forgotten original decor included a summer sky ceiling in green, blue and sunset pink, and a Grecian style interior in blue and silver. The first film – 'O.H.M.S.' had to be shown without the organ, which was eventually ready for Florence de Jong to make her appearance on the 12 September 1938. Being a 2-manual theatrone, it was portable and playable at other Morris theatres. It also visited the Rio after Morris bought that cinema in May 1938. However, when Morris acquired the Rialto, Coventry Street, London, the theatrone went there in 1942 and subsequently in 1947, to the Dreamland ballroom, Margate. The Ritz passed to Essoldo, taking their name in 1962. As their last redoubt, the last Sheerness cinema was able to become a Classic in 1972, but by then the stalls floor was so rotten that circle only operation was called for. Melvin Chilver took over on the 23 May 1977, and used the stalls for an American pool hall. The circle was segregated, and reopened as Woody's (after the street), with 366 seats. This failed to strike a chord, bringing in only 3 to 4 per night. At that rate, the antique projectors were not worth replacing. However, when Jan and Ray Sutton's plans for the Queens, Sittingbourne were thwarted, they channelled their energies

The Oxford, Sheerness, in later 'bingo' days (CTA)

The Argosy, Sheerness on Sea, opened in 1936 (CTA)

George Cole's Rio, Sheerness, in 1937

into saving Woody's. After a year's darkness, the cinema was back as **Images** on the 14 October 1979. Patrons used a bisected entrance with bay window looking into the pool and snooker room from the cinema side. Passing upstairs, the film fan would enter an upper foyer, after noting a thirties mirror halfway up. After paying, they would ascend a few more steps into a largely black auditorium, relieved by spotlights on an unmasked screen. Sheerness remained largely indifferent, and losses of up to £25,000 were incurred. The last show, announced months in advance, played to a half term audience of 36 on Saturday, 9 November 1985. One discerning child asked to see 'Peter Pan' to mark her probably last chance to see a film on Sheppey, as a birthday treat. Half term ended, and the Suttons moved away to a new life in Llangybi, Wales.

Still on Sheppey, the **Beach Hall, LEYSDOWN** once showed films during the summer season. The hall, owned by Leysdown Hotel and Amusements Ltd., first opened in June 1928. It was listed in the 1945 Kinematograph yearbook but an indifferent bus service deterred the author from checking whether the hall was still standing. **QUEENBOROUGH's** former cinema certainly is not, but the site halfway along the High Street next to Fig Tree House is findable. The original building was an adaptation of a Geogian house with the name 'Royal Picture-drome' emblazoned across the top of the parapet. The façade was windowless and had 2 suspended globes. The **Royal** opened in 1912, but it was gutted by fire on the 29 May 1918, despite the best efforts of a party of soldiers and sailors assisting the firemen. Sadly the tide was out that evening! The cinema was rebuilt to the design of Marshall Harvey of Sittingbourne, and reopened as 'Sheppey's super cinema' on the 15 November 1920. Now known as the **Queens**, it held 723 (570 + 153). The ground floor foyer had a ticket office and cloakrooms leading off it, and the box and rewind room were reached from a door halfway up the balcony stairway. There were 2 glass barriers at the back of the balcony (blue seats), whilst those in the stalls (red seats), had a bowl-shaped rake to contend with. The walls had 5 ornamental panels on each side.

Advertising in the press ceased in April 1936, signifying closure, but in October, H. W. Grose, who ran several small Kent cinemas, reopened the Queens after recarpeting and reseating it. The opening attraction was 'Broadway Melody' – presumably not the first talkie to reach Queenborough, it being the 12 October 1936! By the end of World War II the cinema was renamed the **Ace** and run by Charles Crathorn, as was the Walmer cinema. The Queenborough cinema closed about 1954 and made way for a private house.

↺
Queenborough's Ace Cinema
following closure (CTA)

The Classic (formerly Parade), Margate, c.1961 (CTA)

THANET

The Isle is still rich in cinema interest, although some prime buildings were lost by bombing or demolition. Moving west to east, we encounter a 'snug litle bug hutch' in **BIRCHINGTON** (see Adrian Jackson's article in *East Kent Critic*, June 1985). Few cinemas have had so many names as the Public Hall Cinema, opened on the 24 October 1910. The same cinema was the Princess (August 1918–November 1918), the Select until September 1933, the Regent until the 28 January 1936, the **Ritz** until the 9 April 1958 and lastly the Regal. Hemmed in by shops, the cinema on the east side of Station Road had a flat over the tiny entrance, and a small yard to the left into which patrons could exit. It held 300, and once had masses of azelias, rhododendrons and even roses banked up to the ceiling – living decor! The smoke and fug nonetheless needed dispelling by liberal doses of 'June' by an usherette. Sales were confined to the box office, which regulars brought in during the lantern slides for local businesses. Pathe news, cartoons and occasional singalongs helped along by a bouncing ball picking out the words on the screen – this was Birchington entertainment.

Space forced the siting of the box on stilts out in the yard, so ports had to be let into one side wall, with prisms to correct distortion on the slightly askew screen. The handle for cranking the tabs and the dimmer switch were at opposite ends of the box, whilst the Kalee 7s had cardboard front shutters. Projectionists found the place memorable, especially one who fell through the roof void on to the 2/3d's – the hole was never properly mended. Later, R. H. Field, proprietor, 1941–61, rebuilt the box. Originally, there was rear projection. The final show came on the 14 October 1961. After a spell as a bingo club, the Regal (or whatever you care to recall it as) became Trader Pink's Night Spot, and subsequently Sand's Cabaret Club, then the Birchington Club (snooker and bingo).

Nearby **WESTGATE** has a fascinating Edwardian Swiss gothic building in St Mildred's Road. Intended as a town hall, but with a rock maple floor for skating, the building opened in March 1910. Films arrived in May 1912. In the Great War, it was standing room only in the Town Hall Cinema, but facing the other way from today's audience. The transparent screen had rear projection. Sunday concerts ran on the Sabbath, but whist drives, skating, dances and even opera displaced films during the twenties. In 1932, the hall became simply the **Carlton Cinema**, holding 490 for talkies. The screen end was reversed about 1957, when cinemascope was installed. (Simplex heads and Ross arcs with Hewittic mecury rectificers, and RCA sound.) Still an independent, Mike Vickers and Barry Kavanagh spent thousands during the spring of 1982 on continuous wall drapes, 600 yards of carpet, 300 luxury seats, Dolby stereo and on repositioning the screen a little higher up. The Carlton remains a comfortable film venue, a good place to see John Huntley's archive film presentations.

MARGATE had plenty of halls to host the new bioscope, among the earliest being the Salvation Army Citadel, Union Street (then the Forresters Hall), at the turn of the century. From 1910, a wooden shed used by Whitehead's laundry in

Fort Road (east side), was used to show films. So was the garden outside, hence the name **Garden Electric**. This closed by 1914 and became the Fort Road garage by 1925, later Richmond Motors. Of the theatres, the reader is directed to Malcolm Morley's 'Margate and its theatres, 1730–1965'. In brief, the **Hippodrome** (late New Grand, 1898), began to screen epics of the silent film – 'Quo Vadis', 'The Battle Of Gettysburg' for example. Live shows stayed, but in 1929, the theatre opted for the talkie craze. It took 2 weeks to cram everyone in for 'Bulldog Drummond'. Variety returned after the initial rush, but films were back in May 1931. However, the advent of the Regal next door, under the same County Cinema circuit, caused film to cease once more. By the time its neighbour was bombed, the Hippodrome had been closed for 13 months. Films made further comebacks in 1946 and again after cinemascope was installed in 1955. However, the then owners, Allwood Theatres, closed this unprofitable outlet and went out of business themselves in 1958. Margate library marks the site of the Hippodrome. The Theatre Royal, Addington Street, claims to be the second oldest provincial theatre in the land, dating from 1787. Now vacant after 20 years as a bingo hall, the last occupiers did their best to keep it in good repair, and the listed grade II building deserves a fitting use. This smaller 700-seat theatre is of interest here because it courted talkies and called itself the **Kinema Royal** from the 16 January 1933. Rear projection brought 'Tonight's The Night' and more to the 'perfect talkie house' but lack of product for so many local cinemas spelled the end of cinema here by December 1933. A long spell of closure in the war has been exceeded now by the time since live shows last played the boards – 22 years ago.

The **Parade Cinema**, named after its location but now at 8 Fort Hill, was a 600-seat one-floor hall built by C. W. Stanley and W. J. Ballard. The much heralded sliding roof was used to ventilate the irregularly-shaped auditorium. Another cinema ready in time to show George V's coronation, the Parade began on the 26 June 1911. Heavy competition stayed its hand with talkies until April 1930, when British Acoustic sound was installed. One proprietor, W. J. Johns, went bankrupt in the thirties, but the Parade was renovated in 1937 and kept open, like the Plaza, throughout the war for the benefit of the troops. In 1952, we find it is the Classic Repertory cinema, with a special brochure to mark Classic's 'better films' campaign. However, films ceased altogether in 1963, and fulltime Vogue bingo took over in 1965. From July 1979 until November 1981, a 16 mm cinema club operated in premises now well past their best. After their departure, a new occupant eventually arrived, bricked in most of the entrance and now you can file in one at a time – for snooker.

The oldest cinema left in Margate, currently specialising in 'Kids' cinema' is the **Plaza**, High Street. It looks much the same as in 1915, the name being longer – Cinema de Luxe. Designed by Peter Stonham to be of striking height, it has an arched recess with inset entrance taking up half the façade. The Mayor came on the 15 February to see the Gaumont Graphic plus 'The Great Irish Rebellion' – then in full swing. Next February, Movietograph projectors also whirred for children's morning matinees, but 'there was no intention to include variety'. Called the Plaza from January 1930, the Plaza prospered and was hastily renovated inside 18 days at the end of 1936. This would explain the thirties style concealed lighting trough which runs back to the balcony edge, leaving a much earlier ceiling – indeed it is an unusual two era sandwich. In February 1978, John Scotchmer, an ex-Classic man and then running Dreamland cinema, spent £10,000 after acquiring the Plaza – mainly on semi-automatic Kalee 19s, and new seating. Lack of product closes the Plaza periodically, mainly in the bleak mid-winter, but hopefully Disney will achieve what sex films failed to do, namely keep the doors open.

The Margate supers are worth a book of their own, and the R.I.B.A. library's periodicals give them due attention. The Dreamland of today had a forerunner. A surplus railway terminus had been adapted for entertainment use in 1867, most memorably as Lord George Sanger's managerie from 1874. A 1911 advert for the Italian and Zoological Gardens states: 'Feeding time at 4, dancing and skating from 8–11 p.m.' A few pictures in the Hall-by-the-Sea were fleshed out to a 3-hour programme by October 1912. By the 17 May 1923, the **Dreamland Cinema** opened in this hall, at which time it was called the Palais de Dance and suitably furnished with chandeliers and full length mirrors. The first were removed, the second concealed, and 900 patrons sat there unreflected. They had a rake but the 275 by 55-ft length ensured rear projection. The cinema escaped a big fire in the adjacent amusement park, which Margate Estates Co. reopened in May 1931. By then they had bought Dreamland a 2-manual 17-unit straight Noterman organ in 1929 and wired up the hall for sound. The surrounding fire delayed rebuilding or perhaps encouraged it. Phase one included a sunshine café and bars at the Marine Terrace end, plus a 90-ft corridor to the cinema. In phase 2, the old Dreamland came down, closing on the 22 September 1934.

Dreamland II is renowned mainly for the influence the sea front elevation, with its central display fin, had on later cinemas, especially the Odeons. J. R. Leathart and W. F. Granger handled the overall design, whilst J. B. Iles, son of the chairman of Margate Estates, had the interior decoration. The facing of the external walls in cellular rustic bricks in English bond has hardly dated at all. Down the entrance hall, a 30-ft high booking rotunda is still the focus for new arrivals today. The Greek key design on the ceiling here is notable. The auditorium was approached by stairs to a 72 by 44-ft wide stalls foyer, with an entrance at one end to the ballroom, or upwards to a higher circle foyer (72 by 18-ft). A licenced bar and tea room opened off this level. The cinema held 2,050 (1,328 + 722) and charged from 7d to 2/–. Dogs could be minded during the show and cars parked free. The auditorium's glory was the Australian walnut and silky oak dado, decorative and acoustical, and some nymph and sea god figures saved from the old cinema. Pipes from the Noterman joined a new Compton, making an instrument costing £4,850 – enough to buy 5 houses in 1935! Space was ample, the projection room for example being 26-ft long. It had a Brenkert Enarc

83

effects projector for organ interludes and a biunal slide projector with an iris dissolver.

Dreamland opened on the 22 March 1935 in the company of mayor Alderman Pettman and Captain Balfour, M.P. Lewis Gerard was resident organist. Showman Harold Finch soon succeeded Jack Binns in running both cinema and ballroom. Harold ensured the silver jubilee and the cinema's first birthday were celebrated in style, the latter with a 500 lb cake for the patrons. A quieter life began in 1940, the new use for Dreamland being as a government repository. Staff were so busy with essential repairs that the resumption on the 1st of July 1946 passed unceremoniously. The main events from then on were the twinning, under Associated Leisure Ltd of the circle area (now 378 + 376) which permitted bingo in the stalls. The twins opened on the 22 April 1973. A video mini, with aircraft style seating, was added in a former bar during May 1981. This 60-seater was computerised whilst the projectionist manned the Westars and zenons in the twins' box. The Medway Theatre Organ Trust restored the 4-manual 19-unit Compton/Noterman in 1975. Sunday concerts are held, latterly by a different society. A highlight came in 1985 when Lewis Gerard was invited by the M.T.O.T. to return from exile in California to 'play it again Lewis'. The cinema, squash courts etc. are now run by the Dutch company, Bembom Brothers.

The **Regal**, Cecil Square was arguably a more attrctive cinema, but sadly a bomb abruptly terminated its existence. Robert Cromie, again designing for County Cinemas, fitted a tower front with a first floor café into a narrow space. The front elevation was of metal and glass with black terrazzo columns, and a canopy featuring a double row lighting box. The auditorium widened out at the end of the entrance hall, seating 1,795. The design was clean and modern, using fibrous plaster mouldings, lighting troughs, covings and cornices, finished in gold and black speckle, relieved by red. There were splay wall grilles and a red and gold daylight. Seating and proscenium curtains were green, with silver festoons. Heavy carpeting had an abstract design in grey, green and black. Completing the picture, there were polished mahogany handrails, sprays of artificial silk flowers, subtly lit, the sum of thirties taste and cosiness, all soft lights and expectation.

Opened on the 21 December 1934, the Regal predated Dreamland but never traded as an Odeon, although taken into that circuit. A mainly military audience left a full house of 'Kipps' as bombers approached to destroy the auditorium on the night of the 7 September 1941. The destruction claimed the 4-manual 12-rank Conacher organ, designed for County by their musical director, Reginald Foort. Reginald's brother Arthur, managed the Regal. After the war, a blackened looking branch of the National Provincial Bank occupied the front portion (still intact), but now the Square has Margate library on the site.

CLIFTONVILLE, part of Margate but quieter, had the third super, but also started out on the turf. The **Riviera Gardens** in Godwin Road was an open-air cinema in 1911, but the 'silent' films in the old tennis court disturbed the

Margate's Theatre Royal, used briefly for cinema in 1933

Lewis Gerard at the Compton/Noterman organ, Margate Dreamland, 1985 (John D. Sharp)

neighbours. They successfully opposed a music licence, having endured the buzzing generator and gramophone already. A wooden building at Clifton Baths first advertised film shows even earlier – 19 October 1910 – first as the Electric, then **Clifton Cinema**. This old drill hall also booked military bands, and patrons could read news agency wires on the stereoscopic daylight screen. Deemed not worth equipping for talkies, the hall closed in 1929. Opened on the 22 January 1912, the **Lounge Picture Salon**, Northdown Road was 'cool and cosy' (not too cool one hopes!). A twin gabled boarding house and garden had been adapted for the 550-seat Lounge. Its foyer in the French conservatoire style, inspired the name. The cinema pioneer Charles Senior originaly ran the cinema, which had not room to provide a proper stage, but nonetheless prospered. The ceiling of the box directly over the entrance was so low that the 'chief' worked sitting down! Sound came on the 16 November 1929, only 3 weeks after the Hippodrome, but the Super down the road was hitting business.

After closing on the 28 September 1935, the Lounge tried a new tack as the Cameo News Theatre in May 1936, but from the 5 July 1937, features took over and the cinema became **The Cameo**. Requisitioned in the war, the Cameo reopened with 404 seats on the 27 May 1946. The loss of the Astoria was helpful in sustaining this main road house until the 23 December 1969. Subsequently, the cinema has been replaced by three shops. A former dance hall further along the road, but on the south side, is often taken for the old cinema – the white faience front is very misleading.

Ideal working conditions (for chiefs), existed further west along the road, at the junction with Wyndham Avenue. In only 14 weeks, the old Palladium garage was turned by architect E. A. Stone, with some help, into Margate's third super cinema. Faced in Croft stone, the **Astoria** welcomed its patrons into an entrance hall elaborately patterned in terrazzo. The Astoria held 1,305 in an auditorium lit by the then to be expected concealed and reflected lighting. There was room here for an 18-ft deep stage and a 3-manual 5-rank Compton. We do not know if Leslie Lawrence made the building vibrate at the organ, but the traffic did so! The projection box and the screen were suspended from the same heavy beam, and shook in unison! There was a café to be found up the balcony stairs. Although first of the local supers, opening on the 4 August 1934, it was least well suited for the passing trade. Only 25 months after Jessie Matthews had seen her own film 'Evergreen' on the opening night, the organ was moved to the Savoy, Stoke Newington, whose owners, ABC acquired the Astoria in June 1937. Bombing closed the Astoria on 20 July 1940, and the damage was worsened beyond redemption in 3 more raids. Not worth rebuilding, a garage is once more on the site, but not one called the Palladium.

BROADSTAIRS has seen 3 permanent cinemas, the latest being quite a newcomer, as a cinema at least. The **Broadstairs Cinema** was built by Margate, Broadstairs and Ramsgate Electric Theatres in the High Street (no. 23), where Tesco later took root. The architect was Horace Dan, who had already converted the Drill Hall, Cliftonville for the same company. An old photo shows the cinema

◊
*A 1950s view of the Odeon,
Broadstairs* (CTA)

*The Odeon, Ramsgate, under
Classic ownership*

through an arch plastered with stills, and flanked with single-storey shops. Holding around 650, the Broadstairs cinema was in time equipped with BT-H sound, and known as the **Picture House** by 1937. Notable owners were Sax Cinemas, together with the Royalty, whose director was Frederick Salt – reminds one of Saxa Salt! The last owners were Highland Development Trust of London, NW10, who closed the then 'New Picture House' down on the 17 February 1962 with '20,000 Leagues Under The Sea'.

The later **Royalty** in York Street near Dundonald Junction has also disappeared. It had a much more dignified frontage with a proper canopy and leaded arched window above. The architect, P. Levett, incorporated a marble staircase from Chesterfield House, London. The 800-seater was built in 9 weeks, opening on the 15 October 1934. The Royalty was quite grand before the war, with uniformed commissionaire and some live acts, such as Trois and his Mandoliers. The Odeon group took control in July 1935, but relinquished their Broadstairs cinema again in 1938. Heavily damaged in the war, the cinema did not reopen until the 3 August 1950 in the presence of Jack Warner. As in 1935, it was named and run by **Odeon**, but was a victim of one of their first rationalisations in 1956. Forty screens had to go then, Broadstairs' inclusion being met with consternation by the chairman of the council. The council bought the Odeon but sold it to a development company.

The **Windsor Cinema** was built in 1911 to house a museum of armour. It was then called the York Gate Hall, being very close to same. After the New Picture House came down, it became a 16 mm cartoon cinema for a time, but by 1965, was known as the Windsor. Despite a struggle in the early days to pay the rent to the council, it is still with us. The sloping site belies its size. At street level, there is a small foyer and access to a small 29-seat balcony. The remaining 126 seats are downstairs. The proscenium surround is flanked by red curtaining, and several windows have been blacked out. Programmes run once nightly without adverts or sales breaks, whilst outside, similar restraint is demanded by the hall's listed status. The Windsor is Broadstairs' independent and is run by R. H. Field, who formerly had the Carlton, Westgate for 34 years, and the Regal, Birchington for 20. It was he who installed a proper projection room and fire escape at the Windsor, added a rake to the stalls floor and raised the circle floor. An extra door in the foyer was installed to deaden street noise from cars ascending Harbour Street. The box had Ross heads with RCA sound heads and carbon arcs. Mr Field recalls the cinema once tried its hand at being a puppet theatre in season, but was an empty shell when he moved in around 1965.

Nero's 2000 discotheque looks to the future but this interesting building on Marina Esplanade, **RAMSGATE**, dates back to 1877. It was then used for music hall and circuses. One source claims that the hall became the **Excelsior Picture-drome** on the 18 May 1908. Press coverage was scant at this time. We do know that the proprietor was one W. J. Attack, who also ran the shortlived **Cinema Lawn** in Royal Road, West Cliff. An advert appearing in August 1911 claims that the Lawn was 'beautifully sheltered from the wind and open between 8 and

10.30 p.m., weather permitting'. One assumes such grassy entertainment was seasonal, and would certainly have ended during the Great War. The author would welcome more information on the past use of Nero's, in particular clarification about its connection (if any) with the 'Sandvia News Theatre'.

Under cover again, the currently disused **King's Theatre**, up a passage from King Street, opened on the 17 November 1910. The Kings was built on the site of the Red Lion livery stables and was spacious for the day with 700 seats. It was designed by H. Bertram Langham of Broadstairs, with a balcony and high-pitched roof. The interior was decorated in green and gold panelling, with the screen framed in white and gold. Run by Ramsgate & District Popular Amusements, the company later became known as Balexcro Theatres – a composite of Messrs Bawn, Alexander and Crow. It was their only cinema to remain open through the last war. Despite passing to the Highland Development Trust, then Victor Arwas and finally to Classic, the cinema retained much original charm. An attempt at modernisation during which the auditorium was decorated in dark blue, with gold and silver stars, only partially hid the original pillared and rounded proscenium arch. Patrons entered a tiny foyer with paybox at street level, then ascended a staircase to the stalls foyer. A further curved staircase led to a disused balcony supported on cast-iron pillars. Diffused light from 6 stained glass windows was cut off from the auditorium by the barrier wall behind the back row. Although Classic had taken over in June 1978, they also had the former Odeon across the road, and major renovation seemed imprudent. The Kings literally went dark early in November 1982 when a rectifier burnt out. Classic cut their losses and sold out to local businessman, Tom Pearson, who had plans for live theatre. A covenant then prevented films being run in competition with the Classic, but this too has closed now.

Still in 1910, **Shanly's Electric Theatre** opened in the St Georges Hall on the 19 December. The site was George Street, south-east side. Advertising as Shanly's Select Theatre (April 1913), the seating was of the tip-up variety. In 1914, press adverts for the cinema disappear, but resume for the Star, George Street in October. As one source claims this opened the preceding June, with Shanly still the proprietor, it is likely that renovation rather than a transfer of building had happened. A Star syndicate leased the cinema, which was run by Hubert Harwood and A. Waldock. The Star closed by 1927, and became the Ramsgate Town Social Working Men's Club. The projection ports were still visible in club days, which lasted until about 1974. It is now the Star snooker club.

Not surprisingly, the **Queens Electric Theatre** was in Queen Street, south-east side. It had been a constitutional club and post office before the same company as the King's opened a cinema there on the 17 July 1911. Tip-up upholstered seats were not enough, for in the twenties directories periodically describe the premises as 'vacant'. Finally closed in 1927, the cinema was used by the Ramsgate & District Electricity Supply Co. Much grander, S. D. Adshead's Royal Victoria Pavilion Theatre, Ramsgate harbour was opened on the 29 June 1904 by Princess Louise of Argyll. Built in the French Academic style, and still architecturally distinguished, the theatre was offering the Pavilion bioscope by April 1913. If the weather was bad, the screen could be rolled on stage and an impromptu show held. After talkies, the **Pavilion** became a full-time cinema with BT-H sound on the 9 September 1929 and joined the Balexcro group in 1936. The auditorium was remodelled in stadium style and a floating screen installed. The seating capacity was 1,200. The building closed from June 1940 until May 1945, then resumed as a cinema until the 16 June 1951. Live shows came back, but in 1976 Harbour Parade acquired another Roman association for Ramsgate with a Club Tiberius Casino. This is still open.

Sanger's amphitheatre saw a demonstration of Birt Acres and his Royal Kinematograph as early as 1897. The impressive building became the Royal Palace Theatre in 1908, and like the Royal Pavilion, a full-time cinema in the wake of talkies. 'The Singing Fool' was booked from the 15 July 1929. About this time, a 3-manual 6-unit Compton was installed with 2 chambers under the stage. F. Rowland Tims came as guest organist from the Adelphi, Slough on the 30 July 1934. Once again, Balexcro took over in 1936, and war closed the doors. However, the reopening attraction was a summer show. Cinema resumed from October 1951 until Highland Development Trust closed the **Palace** for good on the 29 October 1960. All but some integral shops and a covered access to the pit were swept away, and a supermarket, of late Shoppers Paradise, is marking the site.

Opposite, there stood the **Ramsgate Picture House**. This had been built in place of some shops and an auctioneers. The arched entrance had a tiled surround with variegated patterns at ground level, like some London tube stations. When opened in October 1920, the Picture House held 600, much less than the 1,482 at the Palace. The owners, Ramsgate Picture House Ltd., were liquidated in February 1935, and Balexcro stepped in. Its projection room housed Kalee 8s and Peerless magnarcs. Closed between September 1940 and August 1943, the cinema lasted until the 4 October 1958, when it closed 'for the season'. However, Highland Development Trust sold the building to Tescos, and their supermarket, now Superdrug, took its place.

At the junction of King and Broad Streets, some biscuit-coloured faience tells us that surely Ramgate had an **Odeon**. It did, from the 22 August 1936. Designed by Andrew Mather, it was the only super in town, but Odeon's 18th to open in that year. Horse stables for the fire station had made way for the striking building with its name carried vertically on the fin. It seated 1,568 (1,034 + 534) and was equipped with BT-H sound. Its history resembles that of the Sittingbourne Odeon, namely a Classic lease-out in 1967, and subdivision. This time it was bingo downstairs and the balcony left intact for cinema. The 1982 figure was 534, compared with 629 at the Kings. Despite the subdivision and good programming, Cannon Classic failed to entice enough patrons and put up the Classic for sale, amidst local protests. Closure took place on the 17 October 1985. Ironically, £30,000 had been spent equipping the former Mecca bingo area into a second cinema during June 1983, but enthusiasm soon waned. To fill a void, the 900 seat **Granville** theatre began to show films on Sundays only from May 1986.

TONBRIDGE

Cinemas have dwindled to nil in **TONBRIDGE**, a town that had seven. Still much the same externally is the **Public Hall** (c.1876) at 176 High Street – now a bingo hall. In 1921 J. H. Taylor altered the interior for cinema use, providing a new entrance, crush hall, tea room and 250-seat balcony. The windows remained so that the hall could be deodorised by the sun's rays – 'the finest natural cleanser'. The Public Hall cinema opened on the 18 July with press praise for the red turkey pattern carpeting and 'armchair' seating on old gold. An early attraction – Mary Pickford in 'Suds' was marked by strands of bunting hung from the canopy. Norma Shearer was the star on the screen in December 1926, when a severe fire burnt much of the interior, except for the balcony. Manager, Arthur Dearden had to be rescued from his top floor flat, but ironically, a bottle of paraffin in the paybox did not ignite.

From the 28 December for nearly 2 years, the cinema was under restoration. It reopened on the 13 October 1928, having added a 2-manual 5-unit Christie organ. The plan of the building was not changed, apart from a modified entrance, new ventilation and a new name – **Capitol**. After 5 months of Harold Howell, Fred Bayco became resident organist at only 16, but he in turn moved on to a Gaumont British posting. The organ moved itself to the Forum, Leeds during 1946. Management changed hands – Tonbridge Cinema Co., 1933–39, Kent & Associated Cinemas, 1939–56 and finally Shipman & King. As S&K also had the Ritz, they closed the Capitol when film product ran short. The last audience on the 28 March 1964 saw Kenneth More in 'We Joined The Navy'. There was no charge, and the national anthem was sung as they left. The Capitol was for sale until the bingo club moved in about 1970. As a cinema, the Capitol was not ideal, with a high and narrow screen hard to concentrate on.

Several other older buildings survived for much less time, among them the **Central Picture Hall**, High Street (west side just north of the Little Bridge). This had been a chapel and public hall before. Occasional film shows became fulltime from August 1910, when tip-up seats were bought, and stairs from the gallery into the body of the hall diverted to the entrance, next to Mrs Leonard's coal office. Patrons received a ticket with the order of films numbered on it. You could tell from this when your number was up and you had seen the pictures round. Singing pictures with a live singer, the Gaumont Graphic and children's shows were offered. The latter patrons were given a free bag of sweets. The Great War put an end to all this generosity and the hall became McCowan's house furniture store until about 1935. Burtons, the tailors is on the site today.

Also in 1910, the **Star Cinema**, Bradford Street opened in an old fellmonger's warehouse. It is not to be confused with the Empire Skating Rink opposite, which had opened on the 20 January, for the Star waited until the 9 October. It seated 600 nightly plus twice weekly matinees, under the proprietorship of Charles Wilson, of the Bull Hotel. He was to found many other cinemas, and Augustus Johnson became the resident proprietor by 1911. The screen measured 18 by 16-ft, and apparently the pianist, Miss Skinner, could watch it, play and read her newspaper all at once! The management had to keep their eye on the river Medway, which liked to come in unasked. If seats and piano failed to beat a hasty retreat, the seats could face a spell of drying out on top of the furnace at the electricity works! A music licence was refused in 1914, so that 'in future, turns will not appear'. Reynolds Pictures and Tonbidge Cinemas took on the Star which stayed silent until the 20 October 1930. Both skating rink and cinema went dark soon after each other, the cinema in mid-February 1939. The building survived as a secondhand furnishers until about 1970, but has now been replaced by D.H.S.S. offices.

Avebury Avenue was Tonbridge's 'West End', with 2 enterprises run by 'Buster West', the towns entertainment maestro in the twenties. At nos. 10 and 12, the Kinema de Luxe opened on the 2 January 1914. It was called the **Empire Picture Palace** from May 1915, or the bug hutch. Mr West sat, bowler hatted, in his office, uttering dire warnings to the children who thronged his matinees. They loved to hurl apple cores from the gallery, but these loathsome pursuits ceased in 1932 when the EPP closed with 'Wait And See' on the 21 May. The New Empire Theatre took the stage in September, playing host to the County Players, and acting as a gateway to the West End. Decorum was relaxed after the war, with Chinese nudes and stuntmen. The name was now Playhouse, and the theatre went through 8 lessees between 1954–55. After falling silent that spring, the theatre was acquired for storage and offices by S. Ramsey & Co. from 1958 until demolition about 4 years later. A W. H. Smith Do-It-All stands on the site.

The New Theatre opposite went the other way – to films. It had opened on the 13 June 1921, having previously been a warehouse. Mr West turned it into a 700-seat theatre, with Georgian white decor. The New closed for conversion to a sound cinema on the 31 August 1929, reopened on the 28 October as the **Pavilion Cinema**. 'The Singing Fool' was the first talkie in Tonbridge. The 641-seat Capitol followed on 2 months later. Western Electric sound was wired in every Tonbridge cinema. The white decor had to go, and so eau de nil green panels and pilasters in gold and beige darkened the auditorium suitably for films. A sunset effect was painted on the central ceiling panel, and the proscenium enlarged. Seating was now 656 (416 + 240). As at the Star, ownership passed to A. Reynolds, who had the Pavilion, Dorking, and thence to Lt.-Col. Middleton of Kent & Associated Cinemas. KAC acquired both Pavilion and Capitol in 1939, and decided in wartime to close the former on the 29 March 1941. The final film? – Joan Bennett in 'The Man I Married'. The Pavilion became a postal sorting office for a time, but now the County Library have a new branch on the site.

Last but not least in impact was the **Ritz**, largest and most comfortable of all, and with its own restaurant. The Ritz in the Botany was opened by Union Cinemas in their declining years. Designed by Frank Verity and Samuel Beverley, it was thought to be modern but not garish. Monotonous outside, but better within, the foyer had a wide staircase leading to balcony and café. The auditorium was decorated in terracotta peach and gold in readiness for the 30 July 1937, when 'Splinters In The Air' and 'Isle Of Fury' were presented. So that

The Capitol, Tonbridge, c.1938 (RCHM)

Snodland's tiny but impressive Grand Cinema

children used to the old Empire felt at home, a chums' club ran, with Shirley Temple (who else?) as president. When all Tonbridge cinemas passed to KAC in 1939, the elderly Star closed, leaving Ritz and Capitol to be handed down to S&K (Shipman and King). The latter took over the Ritz in August 1955.

By 1975, as an ABC house, the Ritz was only marginally in the black and on the 14 March 1978 it closed. A Bejam freezer store was carved out of the stalls, heading off a bid from Graylemere Developments to create a 5-screen cinema and restaurant. However, a small 98-seat mini was opened in the old café by South Coast Entertainment Associates. They had planned a second auditorium, but press recation to the Carlton mini was hardly adulatory. Only the screen escaped censure – noisy projection, fuzzy definition, blocked toilets and hideous decor engaged letter writers. The latter was varied to say the least – red seats, blue curtains and red walls and flock wallpaper over the windows. The original lino on the staircase jarred with the blue, white, orange and brown foyer. Under the headline 'Most boring town's cinema to close' the jaded owners stated they wished they had never heard of the place, which they jettisoned on the 25 September 1981. Even the new Sean Connery film, 'Outland' only drew 6 people on its first night. Today filmgoers should try the Medway Hall at the Angel Centre.

SNODLAND was self-contained enough to sustain its own cinema for many years. The **Grand**, Holborough Road, was a plain brick building with an arched front and a gothic style interior painted red with a white roof. The cinema opened as the Snodland Picture Palace on the 23 March 1912, taking in 360 patrons. It was equipped with Pathe projectors. Children were admitted for 2d, inclusive of a packet of popcorn – heating up maize goes back a long way it seems! Mrs Taylor provided spirited piano accompaniment. A mischievous complaint to the Home Office about inadequate fire exits was not upheld – even the rewind room had 2 exits and the cinema could be emptied in 31 seconds, Malling R.D.C. discovered. A talkie was shown in 1924 using synchronised gramophone records, in advance of sound on film. By 1938, the Grand was known as the **Queens** and run in unison with the Strood Queens. However, the new Wardona took away business and the older cinema became a Catholic church.

Harry Ward had founded a chain of 'mini supers' to serve smaller towns and villages with populations up to 6,000. His company, formed in 1933, hoped to build a chain of 20 cinemas, but was to peak at just 4 halls. Being a film distributor, Ward hoped to obtain good programmes, but operating difficulties eventually starved him of product. The first 2 cinemas were to be in Snodland High Street and West Malling (not built). Snodland was erected by W. R. Hindmarsh & Co. of Eltham, and cost £8,000 for a 650-seat one-floor design. A reception was held at the Bull Hotel on the 21 March 1938, followed by music from the Eric Harris Band on the Wardona's stage, followed by the Shirley Temple version of 'Wee Willie Winkie'. The cinema was comfortable if plain, its box equipped by Gaumont British sound. A Mrs Dungate of Snodland coined the name **Wardona** for a £10 prize offered in the *Kent Messenger*. Subsequent history is unspectacular, Snodland's cinema closing as the Savoy in 1963. A bingo club took possession until recently – now there is talk of snooker.

Perhaps the strangest cinema in Kent, albeit a private venture, was one set up in an oast house by farmworkers on **DITTON COURT** Farm. A screen, curtains and projector plus a stack of chairs were acquired, any overflow sitting on hop sacks. The cinema in the oast loft opened in 1949 as a bonus for hop pickers, but no doubt it has fallen beneath the march of the mechanical pickers, like its audience. A photograph survives in the County Library's Springfield local collection, classified under hop farming.

The **Raymar, WEST MALLING**, is an increasingly rare, but well regarded village cinema. The wooden building was erected privately as the Badminton Hall, mainly for that game, but also as a public hall until one could be built. Ray and Mary Halkes moved from Dover in 1951 and converted the hall into a 240-seat cinema. Running by the following January, it was first known as the Badminton Cinema, and then from about 1955 as the Raymar – a blend of Ray and Mary. The Halkes had formed Raymar Cinemas, but this is their only operation. The stage was used until a large immovable cinemascope screen was installed. In 1975, new armchair seating with wider spacing cut capacity to 216. In 1980, a Westrex 7000 tower was bought for the projection room, enabling programmes to run for 4½ hours including the reverse. The quietly sited cinema down Norman Road is near a cricket pitch. There is an adjacent flat for the owners. Patrons are welcomed nightly except Thursdays.

In **BOROUGH GREEN**, a sandpit was filled in to provide the site for the **Electric Palace**. Standing at 25 Wrotham Road, the cinema was one where everyone knew each other and had a favourite seat. Revues, such as one provided by the Gossips in 1923, drew folk from miles around. The projector was powered by gas, petrol and finally electricity. Externally, the pitched roof was replaced by a flat one in 1920. The owners over the years have included W. Gilbert (for whom it was built in 1912) H. Sawdy and G. Downs of Swanley. The latter came here in 1953 and changed the name to **Rex**. The exterior of the Rex was plain, apart from an emergency ladder up to the projection room, and a small oriel window over the canopy. To survive, the last proprietor, Frank Davies, calculated that £5,000 was needed to upgrade equipment and seating. Support did not merit the cost, so just before the doors were due to open for 'Tara's Bulba' on Monday, 2nd March 1964, Mr Davies decided to call it a day. The cinema has subsequently seen a number of light industrial occupants, the current user being an electronics firm. As a postscript, one cinema directory entry in 1945 lists both a Borough Green Electric Theatre and a Palace, both with the same prices and phone number. I have no evidence of two separate buildings in Borough Green, and believe there was just one building in Wrotham Road, 300 seats being about right for 2,000 inhabitants.

The Ritz (now Cannon), Tunbridge Wells, c. 1935 (CTA)

The Regal, Cranbrook, after closure in 1984

TUNBRIDGE WELLS

The Cannon, **TUNBRIDGE WELLS** enjoys a large catchment area in two counties, all competitors having locked their doors. The spa has had 7 cinemas, the first permanent one being in the **Camden Hall**, Camden Street. This stood between Calverley Road and Garden Street, and took films on board during 1909. Next year the hall and adjacent property was altered into a 'pretty bijou theatre' known as the Camden Electric. 300 tip-up seats came in, and the floor was laid with a pile carpet or turkey pattern linoleum. Reopened by Mr F. E. Bellamy on the 12 October 1910, it was a typical 'silent' hall, if you disregard the piano. By 1921 it was run by Messrs Shipman and Wells, but closed in 1925. The premises were divided between a Home & Colonial stores and a domestic stores. These disappeared in the mid sixties.

Further out, a skating rink opened in Culverden Down on the 1st November 1909, next to the Culverden Down Machine Bakery. The rink had 1,000 square feet of floor space with a military band plus instructors on hand daily – 'no gratuities please'. The rink was adapted for cinema with a raked floor and special area for bath chairs, this being a spa town. The **Cinema de Luxe** opened on the 4 August 1913, engaging a small orchestra. Contrary to usual trends, films ceased in the Great War, but skating resumed until 1921. The building became a depository, a warehouse for Nicholl & Co. in the sixties, then premises for Magnet Southern.

Little is known of the third early hall at 97 Camden Road. It was next to the Roebuck public house and had been Harrison's Exchange and Mart. Ambrose Adams converted it into a cinema called the **Picture Playhouse** in 1912, which it remained until 1922. It then became the London & Provincial Temperance Billiards Hall. From 1933–38 a covered market had possession, then after the war a greengrocers. Harrington Candies (confectionery makers) were there from 1958 but more recently car bodies have been repaired under its roof.

The Kozzy in Calverley Road was the first cinema to achieve longevity. Its real name was **Kosmos**, but the nickname suggests that it became a local institution. Opened in 1913 at nos. 40 and 42, the cinema soon established itself with Mrs Beatrice Gilbert accompanying the films from the orchestra pit. Mac Sennett comedies and Tom Mix westerns were the staple diet. Western Electric took the Kozzy into the thirties and Fred Bernhard of Union Cinemas took control of the cinema in about October 1935. After the absorbtion of Union Cinemas into ABC, Bernhard retained control of all the existing Tunbridge Wells cinemas in a separate company (Provincial and Urban Cinemas) until he died of a brain tumour at the age of 46 in June 1949. The Kosmos made its way to the Essoldo circuit. At first many regular patrons dropped in during their afternoon shopping trip, but then the fare changed to X certificates – Bardot inter alia. A lively teenage audience booed the love scenes and cheered the action. Their last chance came on the 26 March 1960 during 'Demetrius And The Gladiators'. Gutted to become a Pricerites, the foyer area is now a Peter Lord shop, and

W. H. Smith occupy the main part of the cinema, whose projection box exit door can be seen bricked up at the back. In the library, a curious cutting describes how a lady passed through a time warp into a curiously old-fashioned café, crowded with silent diners. On returning next day to try out the café, it was not there, and the Kosmos café had returned to its normal time span.

The **Great Hall** was the largest room at the rear of the Public Hall (1870). This French Renaissance style edifice faces the main entrance to the railway station. The hall measured 42 by 100-ft and was large enough to seat 700. 'Positively for 9 days only' West's Pictures brought the heroine of Mafeking here in 1910. However, it was 1920 when E. A. Stone adapted the Great Hall into a full-time cinema. A layer of Wilton carpeting and tip-up seats made the venue comfortable. RCA sound came along later, and the Great Hall Cinema only ceased when Fred Bernhard died. Tunbridge Wells became an Essoldo city, the company re-opening this cinema as a teenage specialist place called the **Roxy**. From the 2 May 1955 until the 8 November 1958 the rock 'n roll generation claimed the hall as their own. 'The High Cost Of Loving' and 'Imitation General' were the last films in this teen epoch. Was it thoughts of rowdyism which lead the Court School of Dancing to reopen with the warning that no teddy boys or people in flamboyant dress would be admitted? The hall was last used as Claridges Night Club, but by 1983 had been made roofless by a fire. In 1985/86 the rest of the building was refurbished for prestige offices, but the hall has vanished.

The **Opera House** (John Biggs, 1902) stands at the other (upper), end of Mount Pleasant. Deceptively large outside, the auditorium seats 750. An illustrated description is given in the 'Curtains' theatres directory (1982). An afternoon bioscope was successfully begun on the 7 October 1910. Although described as 'too good for pictures' by Dr Walford Bodie in 1921, declining patronage forced the theatre to come round 10 years later. The name Opera House was chosen to sound less decadent than theatre, although one wonders what the Edwardians would have made of bingo! L. H. Jackson, of the Kosmos, had a box built at the rear for back projection – it can still be seen today.

The Opera House took the Kosmos route to Essoldo via Fred Bernhard. The latter company were minded to go over to bingo. Rather than risk the building being demolished, the council eventually consented, amidst the inevitable protests. A final play on the 3 February 1968 and the cry of the bingo caller was heard. The caller worked for Ladbrokes until 1986, when their clubs passed to Top Rank. Ladbrokes who leased the building from the ICI pension fund, had tastefully redecorated the interior, and installed aluminium front doors. Ironically, Kent Opera play at the Municipal Assembly Hall, not here. Grade II listed, the building is structurally preserved including the tiers of boxes. For organ historians, I would add that a William Hill/Norman and Beard straight organ was installed between November 1925 and 1929. This was later rebuilt for Dunedin Town Hall, New Zealand.

'Kent's most luxurious theatre' opened its doors at the corner of Mount Pleasant and Church Road on the 3 December 1934. The **Ritz** development included 15 shops flanking the cinema's corner entrance. Robert Cromie's design included a glass tower at the left end of the canopy, which glowed with colour at night. This was removed in the early fifties. Construction only took 20 weeks, with up to 250 men at work. The lavish Ritz included a 3-manual 7-unit Compton organ, costing £7,000, which Alex Taylor guested on the opening night. In the programme too were four films, topped by Gracie Fields in 'Sing As We Go'. One can imagine the scale of pre-war cinema operation by recalling that the staff included 4 projectionists, 4 doormen, 13 usherettes and salesgirls, a page boy, car park attendant and the waitresses in the Florida restaurant. All these and more were employed in a single screen 1,600-seat cinema! The Ritz opened under Tunbridge Wells Entertainments, in association with Union Cinemas. The overblown Union circuit folded and the disillusioned Fred Bernhard retained the 4 Tunbridge Wells cinemas until his death in 1949. The group passed to H. H. Wingate and then in February 1954 to Essoldo. Being their number one outlet, the Ritz became the Essoldo.

Essoldo twinned the cinema in 1970, creating 2 auditoria seating 450 and 366. Concurrently, the Compton was moved to the Regal, Henley, Classic added a low ceilinged 123-seat third cinema in the old restaurant. Patrons now pass the entrance to the bar on the way up to numbers 2 and 3. Modernisation has concealed thirties details such as the organ grilles with their Chinese motifs. The original decor was dull gold, sable and peach, with flame-coloured draperies. Much altered, the **Cannon** reached its 50th anniversary, having admitted 263,000 patrons the year before (1983) as the Classic. One non-standard feature, not to be overlooked, is the ghostly reappearance of a former employee, who lost his balance and was killed whilst trying to change the lettering on the canopy. One hopes the present staff will be changing the film titles in safety for many years to come.

My enquiries about the nature of the Circular Cinema in Stone Street **CRAN-BROOK** have drawn a blank locally, except that it is recorded in directories from 1924 until the Regal surpassed it in 1938. Plans for the latter show a tower feature, to offset its off High Street location, but this was deemed out of keeping. A more modest looking brick-built cinema arose, with rounded windows on the right-hand side visible up the paved approach road. Not unlike its namesake in Henley, this Regal was however designed by a different architect (P. Levett) a year later. The Regal held 460, with space around it for 40 cars. These drove in first on the 13 December 1938. Little press interest marked the opening screening of Anna Neagle in 'Victoria The Great'.

The **Regal** was run by the Senior family, originally the father Charles and then Brian and David Senior of Brighton. For the last two decades, Brian Horsley, who started as a rewind boy in London, kept cinema alive in this little wealden town, together with his wife Violet. For the technically-minded, the box had Kalee 12s and BA duosonic sound. As far as I know, bingo did not run in tandem with films, and so it was a pure cinema which Cranbrook lost on the 2 February 1984. Bond's farewell – 'Never Say Never Again' was poignant as it looked like International

Stores were going to build a larger supermarket on the site.

Two larger villages in the area held regular film shows for a number of years. Those in **HAWKHURST** took place in the parish hall (**Victoria Hall**) which seated 250. Presumably the building termed The Cinema in a 1925 directory refers to this hall. By 1945, the hall was being rented twice a week by A. Alcock of Carlton Cinemas, who booked two different films a week, and charged from 7d to 2/2d for admission. The Kinematograph yearbook has entries up until 1959, but the proscenium arch width of only 14 feet would have been limiting as wide screen presentation became the norm.

The **Royal Victoria Hall, SOUTHBOROUGH** is notable for being the first municipally-owned theatre in the country. Built in 1900 to the design of William Harmer, the original look was chapel-like with a fine cast-iron canopy. Seats were placed on stepped platforms downstairs as needed, or permanently upstairs in the gallery. The hall was used for cinema in the early twenties, and then, once more, after a 50 year gap, on the 14 February 1975. On that day, Bill Pryor of the Plaza, Oxted, with the permission of the Classic, Tunbridge Wells, staged a one-day presentation of 'The Tales of Beatrix Potter'. Between 1977–79, a modernisation programme removed the original canopy and rendered the front elevation in a bland ochre hue.

The Victoria Hall, Southborough, before removal of canopy (CTA)

GAZETTEER

The book is arranged alphabetically by name of local government district, to group neighbouring cinemas together. The one exception is that all the Medway Towns are in one chapter. A district symbol, e.g. DA – Dartford is given after each place entry. Current (summer, 1987) status is given for each cinema, using the following abbreviations:

B – Bingo hall   C – Cinema   C + B – Cinema(s) and Bingo Club   Ch – Church   Dem – Demolished   Der – Derelict   Ind – Industrial use   N – Nightclub, discotheque or casino   Ret – Retail use. Any other use given in full.

Town	Cinema	Present status	Page
ASHFORD (A)	Odeon	B	6
	Palace	Dem	5
	Picture House	C	5
AYLESHAM (DO)	Cinema		32
BIRCHINGTON (TH)	Ritz	N	81
BOROUGH GREEN (TO)	Rex	Ind	95
BROADSTAIRS (TH)	Picture House	Dem	88
	Royalty/Odeon	Dem	88
	Windsor	C	88
CANTERBURY (C)	Canterbury Electric	Restaurant	9
	Central	Dem	10
	Cinema 3	C	13
	Odeon	Theatre	12
	Palais de Luxe	Dem	9
	Regal/Cannon	C+B	12
	St Georges	Dem	9
CHATHAM (MT)	Cinema de Luxe	Offices	45
	Empire	Dem	48
	Imperial	Dem	48
	Invicta	Dem	46
	National Electric	Ret	45
	Palace/Gaumont	Ret	51
	Picture House	Dem	46
	Regent/Cannon	C	48
	Ritz	B	49
CHERITON (SH)	Electric	Dem	66
	St Martins Hall	Dem	66
CLIFFE-AT-HOO (MT)	Globe	Dem	45
CLIFTONVILLE (TH)	Astoria	Dem	86
	Clifton		86
	Lounge/Cameo	Dem	86
	Riviera Gardens		84
CRANBROOK (TW)	Regal	Der	99
DARTFORD (DA)	Gem	Dem	19
	New	Dem	19
	Scala	N	20
	State/Granada	B	20